# THE INNER PLANETS

Edited by
Nicholas Faulkner and Erik Gregersen



Britannica Educational Publishing
IN ASSOCIATION WITH
ROSEN
EDUCATIONAL SERVICES

Published in 2019 by Britannica Educational Publishing (a trademark of Encyclopædia Britannica, Inc.) in association with The Rosen Publishing Group, Inc.
29 East 21st Street, New York, NY 10010



Distributed exclusively by Rosen Publishing.
To see additional Britannica Educational Publishing titles, go to rosenpublishing.com.

**Britannica Educational Publishing**
J.E. Luebering: Executive Director, Core Editorial
Andrea R. Field: Managing Editor, Compton's by Britannica

**Rosen Publishing**
Nicholas Faulkner: Editor
Brian Garvey: Series Designer / Book Layout
Cindy Reiman: Photography Manager
Sherri Jackson: Photo Researcher

**Library of Congress Cataloging-in-Publication Data**

Names: Faulkner, Nicholas, editor. | Gregersen, Erik, editor.
Title: The inner planets / edited by Nicholas Faulkner and Erik Gregersen.
Description: New York : Britannica Educational Publishing, in Association with Rosen Educational Services, 2019 | Series: The universe and our place in it | Audience: Grades 7-12. | Includes bibliographical references and index.
Identifiers: LCCN 2018011821| ISBN 9781508106081 (library bound) | ISBN 9781508106074 (pbk.)
Subjects: LCSH: Inner planets--Juvenile literature. | Solar system--Juvenile literature.
Classification: LCC QB606 .I56 2018 | DDC 523.4--dc23
LC record available at https://lccn.loc.gov/2018011821

*Manufactured in the United States of America*

**Photo credits:** Cover (top), p. 1 Carlos Fernandez/Moment/Getty Images; cover (bottom) Johan Swanepoel/Shutterstock.com; back cover © iStockphoto.com/lvcandy; p. 7 NASA/Lunar and Planetary Institute; pp. 10, 24, 27, 29 NASA/Johns Hopkins University Applied Physics Laboratory/Carnegie Institution of Washington; p. 14 NASA/TRACE/SMEX; p. 21 NASA/JHUAPL/Carnegie Institution of Washington/Science Source; pp. 26, 68 NASA; pp. 36, 59, 61 NASA/JPL; pp. 41, 48 NASA/Goddard Space Flight Center; p. 44 (top and bottom) © Courtesy of C.M. Pieters through the Brown/Vernadsky Institute to Institute Agreement and the U.S.S.R. Academy of Sciences, and C.M. Pieters et al. "The Color of the Surface of Venus," Science, vol. 234, p. 1382, Dec. 12, 1986,copyright © 1986 by the American Association for the Advancement of Science; p. 46 Detlev van Ravenswaay/Science Source; p. 51 NASA/JPL/Caltech (NASA photo #PIA00311); p. 64 NASA/NOAA/GSFC/Suomi NPP/VIIRS/Norman Kuring; pp. 74, 76, 78, 81, 83, 93 Encyclopædia Britannica, Inc.; p. 91 NASA/JPL/Malin Space Science Systems; p. 96 NASA/JPL/Main Space Science Systems; p. 98 NASA/JPL-Caltech/Univ. of Arizona; p. 102 NASA/JPL/University of Arizona/Los Alamos National Laboratories; p. 107 NASA/JPL/Malin Space Science Systems; p. 111 JPL-Caltech-ASU/NASA; interior pages background (blue triangles) DiamondGraphics/Shutterstock.com.

# CONTENTS

## CHAPTER 4

# INTRODUCTION

Broadly, a planet is defined as any relatively large natural body that revolves in an orbit around the Sun or around some other star and that is not radiating energy from internal nuclear fusion reactions. In addition to the above description, some scientists impose additional constraints regarding characteristics such as size (e.g., the object should be more than about 1,000 km [600 miles] across, or a little larger than the largest known asteroid, Ceres), shape (it should be large enough to have been squeezed by its own gravity into a sphere—i.e., roughly 700 km [435 miles] across, depending on its density), or mass (it must have a mass insufficient for its core to have experienced even temporary nuclear fusion).

As the term is applied to bodies in Earth's solar system, the International Astronomical Union (IAU), which is charged by the scientific community with classifying astronomical objects, lists eight planets orbiting the Sun; in order of increasing distance, they are Mercury, Venus, Earth, Mars, Jupiter, Saturn, Uranus, and Neptune.

The planets can be divided into two groups. The inner planets—Mercury, Venus, Earth, and Mars—lie between the Sun and the asteroid belt. The outer planets—Jupiter, Saturn, Uranus, and

This illustration shows the approximate sizes of the planets relative to each other. The inner planets are the first four from the Sun *(left)*, noticeably smaller than the outer planets.

Neptune—lie beyond the asteroid belt. The inner planets, are dense, rocky, and small. Since Earth is a typical inner planet, this group is sometimes called the terrestrial, or Earth-like, planets.

The inner planets, along with the Moon, have average densities in the range of 3.9–5.5 grams per cubic cm, setting them apart from the four outer, giant planets, whose densities are all close to 1 gram per cubic cm, the density of water. The compositions of these two groups of planets must therefore be significantly different. This dissimilarity is thought to be attributable to conditions that prevailed during the early development of the solar system.

The surfaces of the terrestrial planets and many satellites show extensive cratering, produced by high-speed impacts. On Earth, with its large quantities of water and an active atmosphere, many of these cosmic footprints have eroded, but remnants of very large craters can be seen in aerial and spacecraft photographs of the terrestrial surface. On Mercury, Mars, and Earth's Moon, the absence of water and any significant atmosphere has left the craters unchanged for billions of years, apart from disturbances produced by infrequent later impacts. Volcanic activity has been an important force in the shaping of the surfaces of the Moon and the terrestrial planets.

We can learn a lot about Earth from our inner-planet neighbors. Mercury is too hot to retain an atmosphere, but Venus's brilliant white appearance is the result of it being completely enveloped in thick clouds of carbon dioxide, impenetrable at visible wavelengths. Below the upper clouds, Venus has a hostile atmosphere containing clouds of sulfuric acid droplets. The cloud cover shields the planet's surface from direct sunlight, but the energy that does filter through warms the surface, which then radiates at infrared wavelengths. The long-wavelength infrared radiation is trapped by the dense clouds such that an efficient greenhouse effect keeps the surface temperature near 465 °C (870 °F, 740 K). Radar, which can penetrate the thick Venusian clouds, has been used to map the planet's surface.

In contrast, the atmosphere of Mars is very thin and is composed mostly of carbon dioxide (95 percent), with very little water vapour; the planet's surface pressure is only about 0.006 that of Earth. The outer planets have atmospheres composed largely of light gases, mainly hydrogen and helium.

The inner planets are similar to Earth in many ways and in other ways very different. This gives scientists great opportunities to study the nature and origin of Earth.

CHAPTER 1

# MERCURY

The planet that orbits closest to the Sun is Mercury. It is also the smallest of the eight planets in the solar system. These features make Mercury difficult to view from Earth, as the small planet rises and sets within about two hours of the Sun. Observers on Earth can only ever see the planet during twilight, when the Sun is just below the horizon.

The difficulty in seeing it notwithstanding, Mercury was known at least by Sumerian times, some 5,000 years ago. In Classical Greece it was called Apollo when it appeared as a morning star just before sunrise and Hermes, the Greek equivalent of the Roman god Mercury, when it appeared as an evening star just after sunset. Hermes was the swift messenger of the gods, and the planet's name is thus likely a reference to its rapid motions relative to other objects in the sky. Even in more recent eras, many sky observers passed their entire lifetimes without ever seeing Mercury. It is reputed that Nicolaus Copernicus, whose heliocentric

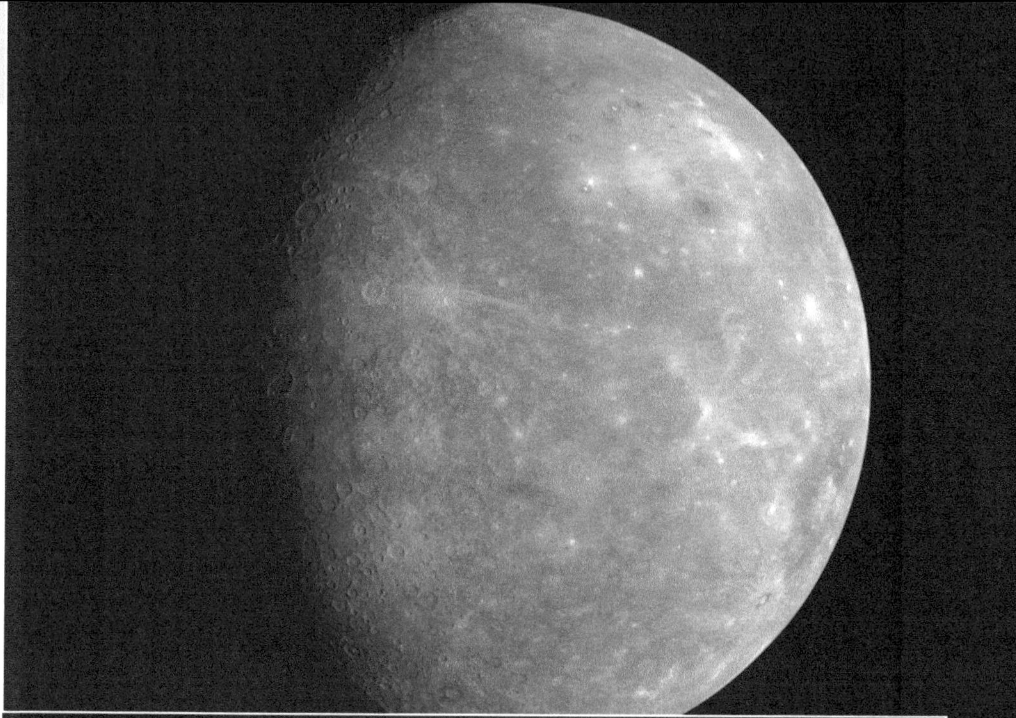

Mercury as seen by the Messenger probe, January 14, 2008.

model of the heavens in the 16th century explained why Mercury and Venus always appear in close proximity to the Sun, expressed a deathbed regret that he had never set eyes on the planet Mercury himself.

## AN INTRODUCTION TO MERCURY

Until the last part of the 20th century, Mercury was one of the least-understood planets, and even now the shortage of information about it leaves many basic questions unsettled. Indeed, the length of its day was not determined until the 1960s, and Mercury's nearness to the Sun gave scientists bound to Earth many observational hurdles, which were overcome only by the Messenger (MErcury Surface, Space ENvironment, GEochemistry, and Ranging) probe. Messenger was launched in 2004, flew past the planet twice in 2008 and once in 2009, and settled into orbit in 2011. It mapped the entire surface of Mercury before crashing into the planet in 2015. Mercury's proximity to the Sun has also been exploited to confirm predictions made by relativity theory about the way gravity affects space and time.

At first glance the surface of the planet looks similar to the cratered terrain of the Moon, an impression reinforced by the roughly comparable size of the two bodies. Mercury is far denser, however, having a metallic core that takes up about 61 percent of its volume (compared with 4 percent for the Moon and 16 percent for Earth). Moreover, its surface shows significant differences from lunar terrain, including a lack of the massive dark-coloured lava flows known as maria and the presence of buckles and scarps that suggest Mercury is shrinking.

Mercury is an extreme planet in several respects. Because of its nearness to the Sun—its average orbital distance is 58 million km (36 million miles)—it has the shortest year (a revolution period of 88 days) and receives the most intense solar radiation of all the planets. With a radius of about 2,440 km (1,516 miles), Mercury is the smallest major planet, smaller even than Jupiter's largest moon, Ganymede, or Saturn's largest moon, Titan. In addition, Mercury is unusually dense. Although its mean density is roughly that of Earth's, it has less mass and so is less compressed by its own gravity; when corrected for self-compression, Mercury's density is the highest of any planet. Nearly two-thirds of Mercury's mass is contained in its largely iron core, which extends from the planet's centre to a radius of about 2,100 km (1,300 miles), or about 85 percent of the way to its surface. The planet's rocky outer shell—its surface crust and underlying mantle—is only some 300 km (200 miles) thick.

## THE CHALLENGES WITH OBSERVING THE PLANET

As seen from Earth's surface, Mercury hides in dusk and twilight, never getting more than about 28° in angular distance from the Sun. It takes about 116 days for successive elongations—i.e., for Mercury to return to the same point relative to the Sun—in the morning or evening sky. This is called Mercury's synodic period. Its nearness to the horizon also means that Mercury is always seen through more of Earth's turbulent atmosphere, which blurs the view. Even above the atmosphere, orbiting observatories such as the Hubble Space Telescope are restricted by the high sensitivity of their instruments from pointing as close to the

Sun as would be required for observing Mercury. Because Mercury's orbit lies within Earth's, it occasionally passes directly between Earth and the Sun. This event, in which the planet can be observed telescopically or by spacecraft instruments as a small black dot crossing the bright solar disk, is called a transit, and it occurs about a dozen times in a century.

Mercury also presents difficulties to study by space probe. Because the planet is located deep in the Sun's gravity field, a great deal of energy is needed to shape the trajectory of a spacecraft to get it from Earth's orbit to Mercury's in such a way that it can go into orbit around the planet or land on it. The first spacecraft to visit Mercury, Mariner 10, was in orbit around the Sun when it made three brief flybys of the planet in 1974–75. In developing subsequent missions to Mercury, such as the U.S. Messenger spacecraft launched in 2004, spaceflight engineers calculated complex routes, making use of gravity assists from repeated flybys of Venus and Mercury over the course of several years. In the Messenger mission design, after conducting observations from moderate distances during planetary flybys in 2008 and 2009, the spacecraft entered into an elongated orbit around Mercury for close-up investigations in 2011. In addition, the extreme heat, not only from the Sun but also reradiated from Mercury itself, challenged spacecraft designers to keep instruments cool enough to operate.

## MERCURY'S ORBIT AND ROTATION

Mercury's orbit is the most inclined of the planets, tilting about 7° from the ecliptic, the plane defined by the orbit of Earth around the Sun; it is also the most eccentric, or elongated planetary orbit. As a result of the elongated orbit, the Sun appears more than twice as bright in Mercury's sky when the planet is closest to the Sun (at perihelion), at 46 million km (29 million miles), than when it is farthest from the Sun (at aphelion), at nearly 70 million km (43 million miles). The planet's rotation period of 58.6 Earth days with respect to the stars—i.e., the length of its sidereal day—causes the Sun to drift slowly westward in Mercury's sky. Because Mercury is also orbiting the Sun, its rotation

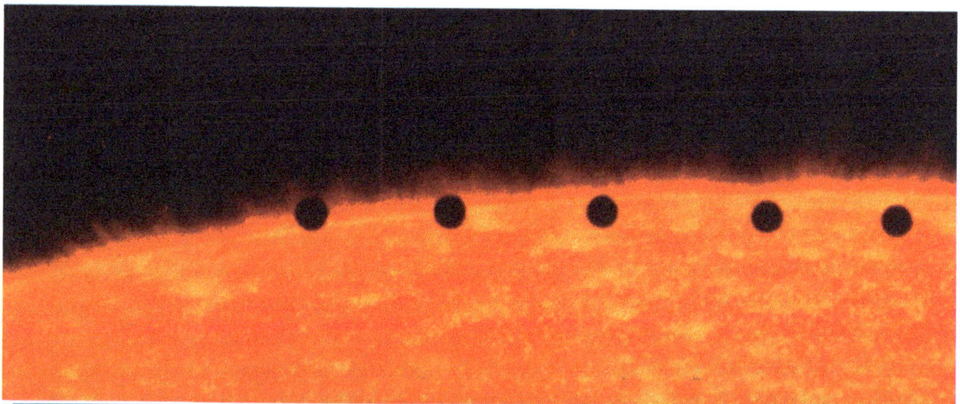

Transit of Mercury across the face of the Sun, a composite of five separate images in ultraviolet light. The time interval between successive images is about seven minutes.

and revolution periods combine such that the Sun takes three Mercurian sidereal days, or 176 Earth days, to make a full circuit—the length of its solar day.

As described by Kepler's laws of planetary motion, Mercury travels around the Sun so swiftly near perihelion that the Sun appears to reverse course in Mercury's sky, briefly moving eastward before resuming its westerly advance. The two locations on Mercury's equator where this oscillation takes place at noon are called hot poles. As the overhead Sun lingers there, heating them preferentially, surface temperatures can exceed 700 kelvins (K; 800 °F, 430 °C). The two equatorial locations 90° from the hot poles, called warm poles, never get nearly as hot. From the perspective of the warm poles, the Sun is already low on the horizon and about to set when it grows the brightest and performs its brief course reversal. Near the north and south rotational poles of Mercury, ground temperatures are even colder, below 200 K (−100 °F, −70 °C), when lit by grazing sunlight. Surface temperatures drop to about 90 K (−300 °F, −180 °C) during Mercury's long nights before sunrise.

Mercury's temperature range is the most extreme of the solar system's four inner, terrestrial planets, but the planet's nightside would be even colder if Mercury kept one face perpetually toward the Sun and the other in perpetual darkness. Until Earth-based radar observations proved otherwise in the 1960s, astronomers had long believed that to be the case, which would follow if Mercury's rotation were synchronous—that is, if its rotation period were the same as its 88-day revolution period. Telescopic observers, limited to viewing Mercury periodically under conditions dictated by Mercury's angular distance from the Sun, had been misled into concluding that their seeing the same barely distinguishable features on Mercury's surface on each viewing occasion indicated a synchronous rotation. The radar studies revealed that the planet's 58.6-day rotation period is not only different from its orbital period but also exactly two-thirds of it.

Mercury's orbital eccentricity and the strong solar tides—deformations raised in the body of the planet by the Sun's gravitational attraction—apparently explain why the planet rotates three times for every two times that it orbits the Sun. Mercury presumably had spun faster when it was forming, but it was slowed by tidal forces. Instead of slowing to a state of synchronous rotation, as has happened to many planetary satellites, including Earth's Moon, Mercury became trapped at the 58.6-day rotation rate. At this rate the Sun tugs repeatedly and especially strongly on the tidally induced bulges in Mercury's crust at the hot poles. The chances of trapping the spin at the 58.6-day period were greatly enhanced by tidal friction between the solid mantle and molten core of the young planet.

## MERCURY'S ATMOSPHERE

A planet as small and as hot as Mercury has no possibility of retaining a significant atmosphere, if it ever had one. To be sure, Mercury's surface pressure is less than one-trillionth that of Earth. Nevertheless, the traces of atmospheric components that have been detected have provided clues about interesting planetary processes. Mariner 10 found small amounts of atomic helium and even smaller amounts of atomic hydrogen near Mercury's surface. These atoms are mostly derived from the solar wind—the flow of charged particles from the Sun that expands outward through the solar system—and remain near Mercury's surface for very short times, perhaps only hours, before escaping the planet. Mariner also detected atomic oxygen, which, along with sodium, potassium, and calcium, discovered subsequently in telescopic observations, is probably derived from Mercury's surface soils or impacting meteoroids and ejected into the atmosphere either by the impacts or by bombardment of solar wind particles. The atmospheric gases tend to accumulate on Mercury's nightside but are dissipated by the brilliant morning sunlight.

Many atoms in Mercury's surface rocks and in its tenuous atmosphere become ionized when struck by energetic particles in the solar wind and in Mercury's magnetosphere. Unlike Mariner 10, the Messenger spacecraft had instruments that could measure ions. During Messenger's first flyby of Mercury in 2008, many ions were identified, including those of oxygen, sodium, magnesium, potassium, calcium, and sulfur. In addition, another instrument mapped Mercury's long cometlike tail, which is prominently visible in the spectral emission lines of sodium.

Although the measured abundances of sodium and potassium are extremely low—from hundreds to a few tens of thousands of atoms per cubic centimetre near the surface—telescopic spectral instruments are very sensitive to these two elements, and astronomers can watch thicker patches of these gases move across Mercury's disk and through its neighbourhood in space. Where these gases come from and go was primarily of theoretical, rather than practical, importance until the early 1990s. At that time Earth-based radar made the remarkable discovery of patches of highly radar-reflective materials at the poles. Messenger later observed that the patches were made of water ice. Despite Mercury's proximity to the Sun, the water ice was able to survive by being covered in an insulating layer of dark organic material in permanently shadowed regions of deep near-polar craters.

The idea that the planet nearest the Sun might harbour significant deposits of water ice originally seemed bizarre. Yet, Mercury has accumulated water over its history, most likely from impacting comets and asteroids. Water ice on

Mercury's broiling surface will immediately turn to vapour (sublime), and the individual water molecules will hop, in random directions, along ballistic trajectories. The odds are very poor that a water molecule will strike another atom in Mercury's atmosphere, although there is some chance that it will be dissociated by the bright sunlight. Calculations suggest that after many hops perhaps 1 out of 10 water molecules eventually lands in a deep polar depression. Because Mercury's rotational axis is essentially perpendicular to the plane of its orbit, sunlight is always nearly horizontal at the poles. Under such conditions the bottoms of deep depressions remain in permanent shadow and provide cold traps that hold water molecules for millions or billions of years. Gradually a polar ice deposit builds up. The susceptibility of the ice to subliming away slowly—e.g., from the slight warmth of sunlight reflected from distant mountains or crater rims—is reduced because it is cloaked by an insulating debris layer, or regolith, about 10–20 cm (4–8 inches) thick, made of organic compounds that also arrived on Mercury in cometary and asteroidal impacts.

## THE PLANET'S MAGNETIC FIELD AND MAGNETOSPHERE

As closely as Mariner 10's measurements could determine, Mercury's magnetic field, though only 1 percent as strong as Earth's, resembles Earth's field in being roughly dipolar and oriented along the planet's axis of rotation. While the existence of the field might conceivably have some other explanation—such as, for example, remanent magnetism, the retained imprint of an ancient magnetic field frozen into the rocks during crustal cooling—most researchers became convinced that it is produced, like Earth's field, by a magnetohydrodynamic dynamo mechanism involving motions within an electrically conducting fluid in the outer portions of Mercury's iron-sulfur core. Measurements by Messenger's magnetometer, made during the spacecraft's first flyby in January 2008, confirm that Mercury's magnetic field is basically dipolar. They fail to reveal any crustal contributions that might be expected from remanent magnetism, so it seems clear that Mercury's dynamo is currently operating.

Mercury's magnetic field holds off the solar wind with a teardrop-shaped bubble, or magnetosphere, whose rounded end extends outward toward the Sun about one planetary radius from the surface. This is only about 5 percent of the sunward extent of Earth's magnetosphere. The planet's atmosphere is so thin that no equivalent to Earth's ionosphere exists at Mercury. Indeed, calculations suggest that on occasion the solar wind is strong enough to push the sunward boundary (magnetopause) of the magnetosphere beneath Mercury's surface. Under these conditions solar wind ions would impinge directly on those portions of Mercury's surface immediately beneath the Sun. Even infrequent occurrences of such an event could dramatically alter the atomic composition of surface constituents.

## THE SURFACE OF MERCURY

The portions of Mercury imaged by Mariner 10 and Messenger look superficially like the Moon. Mercury is heavily pockmarked with impact craters of all sizes. Interspersed among the larger craters are relatively flat, less-cratered regions termed "intercrater plains." These are similar to but much more pervasive than the light-coloured plains that occupy intercrater areas on the heavily cratered highlands of the Moon. There are also some sparsely cratered regions called smooth plains, many of which surround

Mercury's north pole.

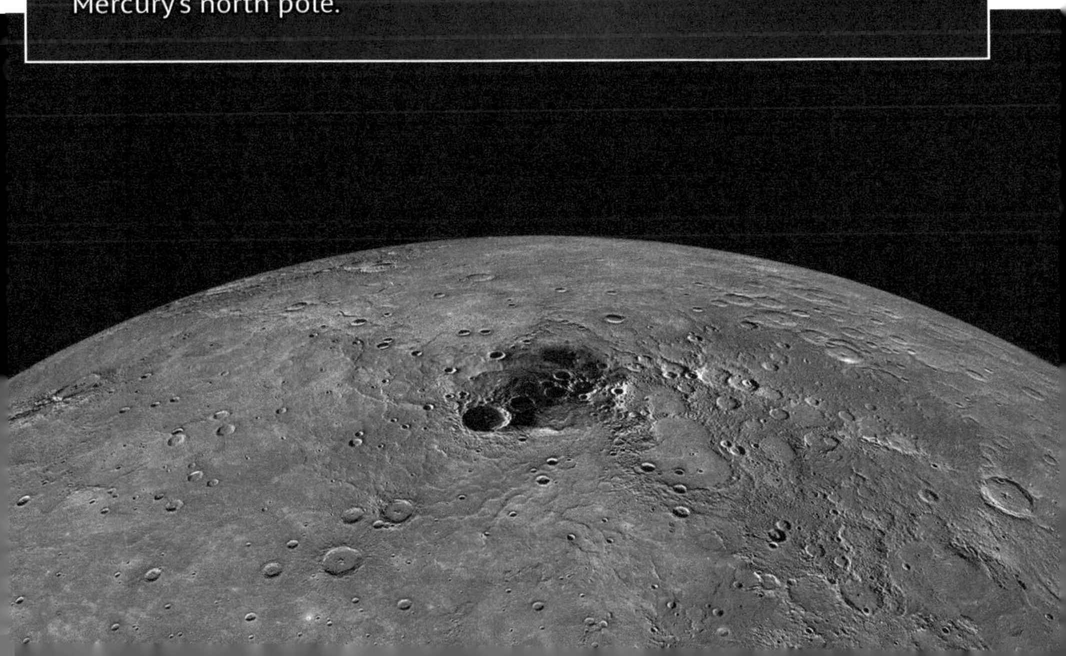

the most prominent impact structure on Mercury, the immense impact basin known as Caloris, only half of which was in sunlight during the Mariner 10 encounters but which was fully revealed by Messenger during its first flyby of Mercury in January 2008.

The most common topographic features on Mercury are the craters that cover much of its surface. Although lunarlike in general appearance, Mercurian craters show interesting differences when studied in detail.

Mercury's surface gravity is more than twice that of the Moon, partly because of the great density of the planet's huge iron-sulfur core. The higher gravity tends to keep material ejected from a crater from traveling as far—only 65 percent of the distance that would be reached on the Moon. This may be one factor that contributes to the prominence on Mercury of secondary craters—those craters made by impact of the ejected material, as distinct from primary craters formed directly by asteroid or comet impacts. The higher gravity also means that the complex forms and structures characteristic of larger craters—central peaks, slumped crater walls, and flattened floors—occur in smaller craters on Mercury (minimum diameters of about 10 km [6 miles]) than on the Moon (about 19 km [12 miles]). Craters smaller than these minimums have simple bowl shapes.

Mercury's craters also show differences from those on Mars, although the two planets have comparable surface gravities. Fresh craters tend to be deeper on Mercury than craters of the same size on Mars; this may be because of a lower content of volatile materials in the Mercurian crust or higher impact velocities on Mercury (since the velocity of an object in solar orbit increases with its nearness to the Sun).

Craters on Mercury larger than about 100 km (60 miles) in diameter begin to show features indicative of a transition to the "bull's-eye" form that is the hallmark of the largest impact basins. These latter structures, called multiring basins and measuring 300 km (200 miles) or more across, are products of the most-energetic impacts. Several dozen multiring basins were tentatively recognized on the imaged portion of Mercury; Messenger images and laser altimetry contributed greatly to the understanding of these remnant scars from early asteroidal bombardment of Mercury.

On the other side of the planet, exactly 180° opposite Caloris, is a region of weirdly contorted terrain. It is interpreted to have been formed at the same time as the Caloris impact by the focusing of seismic waves from that event to the antipodal area on Mercury's surface. Termed "hilly and lineated terrain," it is an extensive area of elevations and depressions. The crudely polygonal hills are 5–10 km (3–6 miles) wide and up to 1.5 km (1 mile) high. Preexisting crater rims have been disrupted into hills and fractures by the seismic process that created the terrain. Some of

The surface of Mercury, as photographed by the Messenger spacecraft on March 29, 2011.

these craters have smooth floors that have not been disrupted, which suggests a later infilling of material.

## PLAINS

Plains—relatively flat or smoothly undulating surfaces—are ubiquitous on Mercury and the other terrestrial planets. They represent a canvas on which other landforms develop. The covering or destruction of a rough topography and the creation of a smoother surface is called resurfacing, and plains are evidence of this process.

There are at least three ways that planets are resurfaced, and all three may have had a role in creating Mercury's plains. One way, raising the temperature, reduces the strength of the crust and its ability to retain high relief; over millions of years the mountains sink and the crater floors rise. A second way involves the flow of material toward lower elevations under the influence of gravity; the material eventually collects in depressions and fills to higher levels as more volume is added. Flows of lava from the interior behave in this manner. A third way is for fragments of material to be deposited on a surface from above, first mantling and eventually obliterating the rough topography. Blanketing by impact crater ejecta and by volcanic ash are examples of this mechanism.

Some of the evidence tilting toward the volcanism hypothesis for the formation of many of the plains surrounding Caloris has already been described. Other comparatively youthful plains on Mercury, which were especially prominent in regions illuminated by a low Sun during Messenger's first flyby, show prominent features of volcanism. For example, several older craters appear to have been "filled to the brim" by lava flows, very much like lava-filled craters on the Moon and Mars. However, the widespread intercrater plains on Mercury are more difficult to evaluate. Since they are older, any obvious volcanoes or other volcanic features may have been eroded or otherwise obliterated, making a definitive determination more difficult. Understanding these older plains is important, since they seem to be implicated in erasing a larger fraction of craters 10–30 km (6–20 miles) in diameter on Mercury as compared with the Moon.

## SCARPS

The most important landforms on Mercury for gaining insight into the planet's otherwise largely unseen interior

The Caloris Basin (in yellow) on Mercury, as seen from the Messenger spacecraft, 2008.

workings have been its hundreds of lobate scarps. These cliffs vary from tens to over a 1,000 km in length and from about 100 metres (330 feet) to 3 km (2 miles) in altitude. Viewed from above, they have curved or scalloped edges, hence the term "lobate." It is clear that they were formed from fracturing, or faulting, when one portion of the surface was thrust up and overrode the adjacent terrain. On Earth such thrust faults are limited in extent and result from local horizontal compressive (squeezing) forces in the crust. On Mercury, however, these features range across all of the surface that has been imaged so far, which implies that Mercury's crust must have contracted globally in the past. From the numbers and geometries of the lobate scarps, it appears that the planet shrank in diameter by as much as 7 km (4 miles).

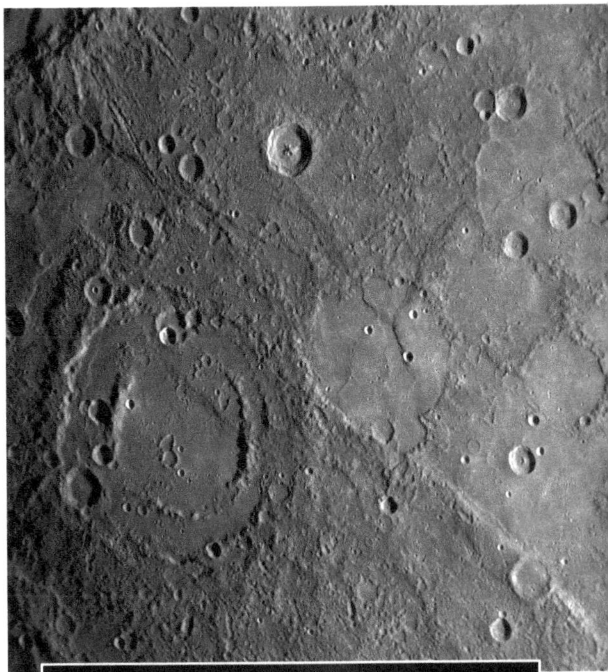

A double-ringed crater on Mercury filled with plains material, in an image taken by the Messenger probe on January 14, 2008.

Moreover, the shrinkage must have continued until comparatively recently in Mercury's geologic history—that is, since the time Caloris formed—because some lobate scarps have altered the shapes of some fresh-appearing (hence comparatively young) impact craters. The slowing of the planet's initial high rotation rate by tidal forces would have produced compression in Mercury's equatorial latitudes. The globally distributed lobate scarps, however, suggest another explanation: later cooling of the planet's mantle, perhaps combined with freezing of part of its once totally molten core, caused the interior to shrink and the cold surface crust to buckle. In fact, many small geologically young scarps have been found, which suggests that the planet has not finished shrinking.

## THE COMPOSITION OF THE SURFACE

Messenger used X-ray fluorescence spectra to study the surface composition of Mercury. It found a high ratio of magnesium to silicon and low ratios of aluminum and calcium to silicon, which showed that the crust was not rich in feldspar like that of the Moon. The surface is rich in sulfur, about 20 times richer than the surfaces of Earth, the Moon, and Mars. Messenger also found low surface abundances of titanium and iron. Mercury seems to have formed in conditions much more reducing—i.e., those in which oxygen was scarce—than other terrestrial planets.

## THE PLANET'S LATER DEVELOPMENT

Planetary scientists continue to puzzle over the ages of the major geologic and geophysical events that took place on Mercury after its formation. On the one hand, it is tempting to model the planet's history after that of the Moon, whose chronology has been accurately dated from the rocks returned by the U.S. Apollo manned landings and Soviet Luna robotic missions. By analogy, Mercury would have had a similar history, but one in which the planet cooled off and became geologically inactive shortly after the Caloris impact rather than experiencing persistent volcanism for hundreds of millions of years, as did the Moon.

On the presumption that Mercury's craters were produced by the same populations of remnant planetary building blocks (planetesimals), asteroids, and comets that struck the Moon, most of the craters would have formed before and during an especially intense period of bombardment in the inner solar system, which on the Moon is well documented to have ended about 3.8 billion years ago. Caloris presumably would have formed about that time, representing the final chapter in Mercury's geologic history, apart from occasional cratering.

A scarp on Mercury. The scarp *(upper left)* curves downward, ending in the large impact crater at the bottom. The region shown is about 200 km (120 miles) across.

On the other hand, there are many indications that Mercury is very much geologically alive even today. Its dipolar field seems to require a core that is still at least partially molten in order to sustain the magnetohydrodynamic dynamo. Indeed, recent measurements of Mercury's gravitational field by Messenger have

## HOW MERCURY FORMED

Scientists once thought that Mercury's richness in iron compared with the other terrestrial planets' could be explained by its accretion from objects made up of materials derived from the extremely hot inner region of the solar nebula, where only substances with high freezing temperatures could solidify. The more volatile elements and compounds would not have condensed so close to the Sun. Modern theories of the formation of the solar system, however, discount the possibility that an orderly process of accretion led to progressive detailed differences in planetary chemistry with distance from the Sun. Rather, the components of the bodies that accreted into Mercury likely were derived from a wide part of the inner solar system. Indeed, Mercury itself may have formed anywhere from the asteroid belt inward; subsequent gravitational interactions among the many growing protoplanets could have moved Mercury around.

Some planetary scientists have suggested that during Mercury's early epochs, after it had already differentiated (chemically separated) into a less-dense crust and mantle of silicate rocks and a denser iron-rich core, a giant collision stripped away much of the planet's outer layers, leaving a body dominated by its core. This event would have been similar to the collision of a Mars-sized object with Earth that is thought to have formed the Moon.

Nevertheless, such violent, disorderly planetary beginnings would not necessarily have placed the inherently densest planet closest to the Sun. Other processes may have been primarily responsible for Mercury's high density. Perhaps the materials that eventually formed Mercury experienced a preferential sorting of heavier metallic particles from lighter silicate ones because of aerodynamic drag by the gaseous solar nebula. Perhaps, because of the planet's nearness to the hot early Sun, its silicates were preferentially vaporized and lost.

Each of these scenarios predicts different bulk chemistries for Mercury. In addition, infalling asteroids, meteoroids, and comets and implantation of solar wind particles have been augmenting or modifying the surface and near-surface materials on Mercury for billions of years. Because these materials are the ones most readily analyzed by telescopes and spacecraft, the task of extrapolating backward in time to an understanding of ancient Mercury, and the processes that subsequently shaped it, is formidable.

been interpreted as proving that at least the outer core is still molten. In addition, as suggested above, Mercury's scarps show evidence that the planet may not have completed its cooling and shrinking.

There are several approaches to resolving this apparent contradiction between a planet that died geologically before the Moon did and one that is still alive. One hypothesis is that most of Mercury's craters are younger than those on the Moon, having been formed by impacts from so-called vulcanoids—the name bestowed on a hypothetical remnant population of asteroid-sized objects orbiting the Sun inside Mercury's orbit—that would have cratered Mercury over the planet's age. In this case Caloris, the lobate scarps, and other features would be much younger than 3.8 billion years, and Mercury could be viewed as a planet whose surface has only recently become inactive and whose warm interior is still cooling down. No vulcanoids have yet been discovered, however, despite a number of searches for them. Moreover, objects orbiting the Sun so closely and having such high relative velocities could well have been broken up in catastrophic collisions with each other long ago.

A more likely solution to Mercury's thermal conundrum is that the outer shell of Mercury's iron core remains molten because of contamination, for instance, with a small proportion of sulfur, which would lower the melting point of the metal, and of radioactive potassium, which would augment production of heat. Also, the planet's interior may have cooled more slowly than previously calculated as a result of restricted heat transfer. Perhaps the contraction of the planet's crust, so evident about the time of formation of Caloris, pinched off the volcanic vents that had yielded such prolific volcanism earlier in Mercury's history. In this scenario, despite present-day Mercury's lingering internal warmth and churnings, surface activity ceased long ago, with the possible exception of a few thrust faults as the planet continues slowly to contract.

CHAPTER 2

# VENUS

Venus is the second planet from the Sun. After the Moon, Venus is the most brilliant natural object in the nighttime sky. It is the closest planet to Earth, and it is also the most similar to Earth in size, mass, volume, and density. These similarities suggest that the two planets may have had similar histories. Scientists are thus intrigued by the question of why Venus and Earth are now so different.

Venus was one of the five planets—along with Mercury, Mars, Jupiter, and Saturn—known in ancient times, and its motions were observed and studied for centuries prior to the invention of advanced astronomical instruments. Its appearances were recorded by the Babylonians, who equated it with the goddess Ishtar, about 3000 BCE, and it also is mentioned prominently in the astronomical records of other ancient civilizations, including those of China, Central America, Egypt, and Greece.

Like the planet Mercury, Venus was known in ancient

Greece by two different names—Phosphorus when it appeared as a morning star and Hesperus when it appeared as an evening star. Its modern name comes from the Roman goddess of love and beauty (the Greek equivalent being Aphrodite), perhaps because of the planet's luminous jewel-like appearance.

## UNDERSTANDING VENUS

Venus has been called Earth's twin because of the similarities in their masses, sizes, and densities and their similar relative locations in the solar system. Because they presumably formed in the solar nebula from the same kind of rocky planetary building blocks, they also likely have similar overall chemical compositions. Early telescopic observations of the planet revealed a perpetual veil of clouds, suggestive of a substantial atmosphere and leading to popular speculation that Venus was a warm, wet world, perhaps similar to Earth during its prehistoric age of swampy carboniferous forests and abundant life. Scientists now know, however, that Venus and Earth have evolved surface conditions that could hardly be more different. Venus is extremely hot, dry, and in other ways so forbidding that it is improbable that life as it is understood on Earth could have developed there. One of scientists' major goals in studying Venus is to understand how its harsh conditions

Venus photographed in ultraviolet light by the Pioneer Venus Orbiter (Pioneer 12) spacecraft, February 26, 1979.

came about, which may hold important lessons about the causes of environmental change on Earth.

Viewed through a telescope, Venus presents a brilliant yellow-white, essentially featureless face to the observer. Its obscured appearance results from the surface of the planet being hidden from sight by a continuous and permanent cover of clouds. Features in the clouds are difficult to see in visible light. When observed at ultraviolet wavelengths, the clouds exhibit distinctive dark markings, with complex swirling patterns near the equator and global-scale bright and dark bands that are V-shaped and open toward the west. Because of the all-enveloping clouds, little was known about Venus's surface, atmosphere, and evolution before the early 1960s, when the first radar observations were undertaken and spacecraft made the first flybys of the planet.

Venus orbits the Sun at a mean distance of 108 million km (67 million miles), which is about 0.7 times Earth's distance from the Sun. It has the least eccentric orbit of any planet, with a deviation from a perfect circle of only about 1 part in 150. Consequently, its distances at perihelion and aphelion (i.e., when it is nearest and farthest from the Sun, respectively) vary little from the mean distance. The period of its orbit—that is, the length of the Venusian year—is 224.7 Earth days. As Venus and Earth revolve around the Sun, the distance between them varies from a minimum of about 42 million km (26 million miles) to a maximum of about 257 million km (160 million miles).

Because Venus's orbit lies within Earth's, the planet exhibits phases like those of the Moon when viewed from Earth. In fact, the discovery of these phases by the Italian scientist Galileo in 1610 was one of the most important in the history of astronomy. In Galileo's day the prevailing model of the universe was based on the assertion by the Greek astronomer Ptolemy almost 15 centuries earlier that all celestial objects revolve around Earth. Observation of the phases of Venus was inconsistent with this view but was consistent with the Polish astronomer Nicolaus Copernicus's idea that the solar system is centred on the Sun. Galileo's observation of the phases of Venus provided the first direct observational evidence for Copernican theory.

The rotation of Venus on its axis is unusual in both its direction and its speed. The Sun and most of the planets in the solar system rotate in a counterclockwise direction when viewed from above their north poles; this direction is called direct, or prograde. Venus, however, rotates in the opposite, or retrograde, direction. Were it not for the planet's clouds, an observer on Venus's surface would see the Sun rise in the west and set in the east.

Venus spins very slowly, taking about 243 Earth days to complete one rotation with respect to the stars—the length of its sidereal day. Venus's spin and orbital periods are very nearly synchronized with Earth's orbit such that, when the two planets are at their closest, Venus presents almost the same face toward Earth. The reasons for this are complex and have to do with the gravitational interactions of Venus, Earth, and the Sun, as well as the effects of Venus's massive rotating atmosphere.

Because Venus's spin axis is tilted only about 3° toward the plane of its orbit, the planet does not have appreciable seasons. Also, Venus's rotational period slowed by 6.5 minutes between two sets of measurements taken in 1990–92 and 2006–08. Astronomers as yet have no satisfactory explanation for Venus's peculiar rotational characteristics. The idea cited most often is that, when Venus was forming from the accretion of planetary building blocks (planetesimals), one of the largest of these bodies collided with the proto-Venus in such a way as to tip it over and possibly slow its spin as well.

Venus's mean radius is 6,051.8 km (3,760.4 miles), or about 95 percent of Earth's at the Equator, while its mass is 4.87 × 1024 kg, or 81.5 percent that of Earth. The similarities to Earth in size and mass produce a similarity in density—5.24 grams per cubic centimetre for Venus, compared with 5.52 for Earth. They also result in a comparable surface gravity—humans standing on Venus would possess nearly 90 percent of their weight on Earth. Venus is more nearly spherical than most planets. A planet's rotation generally causes a bulging at the equator and a slight flattening at the poles, but Venus's very slow spin allows it to maintain its highly spherical shape.

## VENUS'S ATMOSPHERE

Venus has the most massive atmosphere of the terrestrial planets, which include Mercury, Earth, and Mars. Its gaseous envelope is composed of more than 96 percent carbon dioxide and 3.5 percent molecular nitrogen. Trace amounts of other gases are present, including carbon monoxide, sulfur dioxide, water vapour, argon, and helium. The atmospheric pressure at the planet's surface varies with surface elevation; at the elevation of the planet's mean radius it is about 95 bars, or 95 times the atmospheric pressure at

Earth's surface. This is the same pressure found at a depth of about 1 km (0.6 mile) in Earth's oceans.

Venus's upper atmosphere extends from the fringes of space down to about 100 km (60 miles) above the surface. There the temperature varies considerably, reaching a maximum of about 300–310 kelvins (K; 80–98 °F, 27–37 °C) in the daytime and dropping to a minimum of 100–130 K (−280 to −226 °F, −173 to −143 °C) at night. At about 125 km (78 miles) above the surface is a very cold layer with a temperature of about 100 K. In the middle atmosphere the temperature increases smoothly with decreasing altitude, from about 173 K (−148 °F, −100 °C) at 100 km above the surface to roughly 263 K (14 °F, −10 °C) at the top of the continuous cloud deck, which lies at an altitude of more than 60 km (37 miles). Below the cloud tops the temperature continues to increase sharply through the lower atmosphere, or troposphere, reaching 737 K (867 °F, 464 °C) at the surface at the planet's mean radius. This temperature is higher than the melting point of lead or zinc.

The clouds that enshroud Venus are enormously thick. In addition, thin hazes exist above and below the main clouds. The upper haze is somewhat thicker near the poles than in other regions. The main cloud deck is formed of three layers. All of them are quite tenuous—an observer in even the densest cloud regions would be able to see objects at distances of several kilometres. The opacity of the clouds varies rapidly with space and time, which suggests a high level of meteorologic activity.

Radio waves characteristic of lightning have been observed in Venus's clouds. The clouds are bright and yellowish when viewed from above, reflecting roughly 85 percent of the sunlight striking them. The material responsible for the yellowish colour has not been confidently identified.

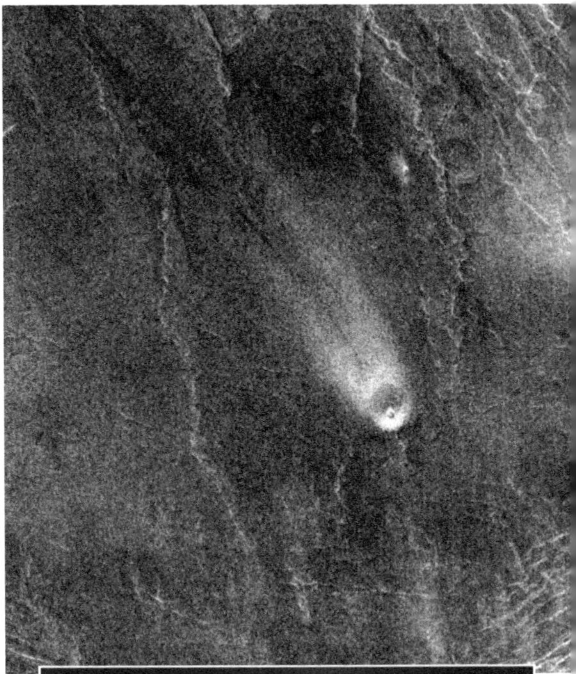

A wind streak on the side of a small volcano on Venus. The volcano is about 5 km (3 miles) in diameter, and the wind streak is about 35 km (22 miles) long.

The microscopic particles that make up the Venusian clouds consist of liquid droplets and perhaps also solid crystals. The dominant material is highly concentrated sulfuric acid. Other materials that may exist there include solid sulfur, nitrosylsulfuric acid, and phosphoric acid.

The circulation of Venus's atmosphere is quite remarkable and is unique among the planets. Although the planet rotates only three times in two Earth years, the cloud features in the atmosphere circle Venus completely in about four days. The wind at the cloud tops blows from east to west at a velocity of about 100 metres per second (360 km [220 miles] per hour). This enormous velocity decreases markedly with decreasing height such that winds at the planet's surface are quite sluggish—typically no more than 1 metre per second (less than 4 km [2.5 miles] per hour). Much of the detailed nature of the westward flow above the cloud tops can be attributed to tidal motions induced by solar heating. Nevertheless, the fundamental cause of this "superrotation" of Venus's dense atmosphere is unknown, and it remains one of the more intriguing mysteries in planetary science.

Most information about wind directions at the planet's surface comes from observations of wind-blown materials. Despite low surface-wind velocities, the great density of Venus's atmosphere enables these winds to move loose fine-grained materials, producing surface features that have been seen in radar images. Some features resemble sand dunes, while others are "wind streaks" produced by preferential deposition or erosion downwind from topographic features. The directions assumed by the wind-related features suggest that in both hemispheres the surface winds blow predominantly toward the equator. This pattern is consistent with the idea that simple hemispheric-scale circulation systems called Hadley cells exist in the Venusian atmosphere. According to this model, atmospheric gases rise upward as they are heated by solar energy at the planet's equator, flow at high altitude toward the poles, sink to the surface as they cool at higher latitudes, and flow toward the equator along the planet's surface until they warm and rise again. Some deviations from the equatorward flow pattern are observed on regional scales. They may be caused by the influence of topography on wind circulation.

A major consequence of Venus's massive atmosphere is that it produces an enormous greenhouse effect, which intensely heats the planet's surface. Because of its bright continuous cloud cover, Venus actually absorbs less of the Sun's light than does Earth. Nevertheless, the sunlight that does penetrate the clouds is absorbed both in the lower atmosphere and at the surface. The surface and the gases of the lower atmosphere, which are heated by the absorbed light, reradiate this energy at infrared wavelengths.

On Earth most reradiated infrared radiation escapes back into space, which allows Earth to maintain a reasonably cool surface temperature. On Venus, in contrast, the dense carbon dioxide atmosphere and the thick cloud layers trap much of the infrared radiation. The trapped radiation heats the lower atmosphere further, ultimately raising the surface temperature by hundreds of degrees.

Study of the Venusian greenhouse effect has led to an improved understanding of the more subtle but very

The surface of Venus, taken by the Venera 13 lander. The top image was taken in natural light. The bottom image was colour corrected to simulate the view in white light.

important influence of greenhouse gases in Earth's atmosphere and a greater appreciation of the effects of energy use and of other human activities on Earth's energy balance.

Above the main body of the Venusian atmosphere lies the ionosphere. As its name implies, the ionosphere is composed of ions, or charged particles, produced both by absorption of ultraviolet solar radiation and by the impact of the solar wind—the flow of charged particles streaming outward from the Sun—on the upper atmosphere. The primary ions in the Venusian ionosphere are forms of oxygen ($O^+$ and $O_2^+$) and carbon dioxide ($CO_2^+$).

## THE SURFACE OF VENUS

The high atmospheric pressure, the low wind velocities,

and, in particular, the extremely high temperatures create a surface environment on Venus that is markedly different from any other in the solar system. A series of landings by robotic Soviet spacecraft in the 1970s and early '80s provided detailed data on surface composition and appearance. Views of the Venusian landscape, typified in colour images obtained by the Soviet Union's Venera 13 lander in 1982 show rocky plains that stretch toward the horizon. Despite the heavy cloud cover, the surface is well illuminated by the yellow-orange light that filters through the clouds.

The most striking characteristic of the surface at the Venera 13 site and most other Venera landing sites is the flat, slabby, layered nature of the rocks. Both volcanic and sedimentary rocks on Earth can develop such an appearance under appropriate conditions, but the reason that the Venusian rocks have done so is not known with certainty. Also present among the rocks is a darker, fine-grained soil. The grain size of the soil is unknown, but some of it was fine enough to be lifted briefly into the atmosphere by the touchdown of the Venera lander, which suggests that some grains are no more than a few tens of micrometres in diameter. Scattered throughout the soil and atop the rocks are pebble-size particles that could be either small rocks or clods of soil.

The general surface appearance at the Venera landing sites is probably common on Venus, but it is likely not rep-

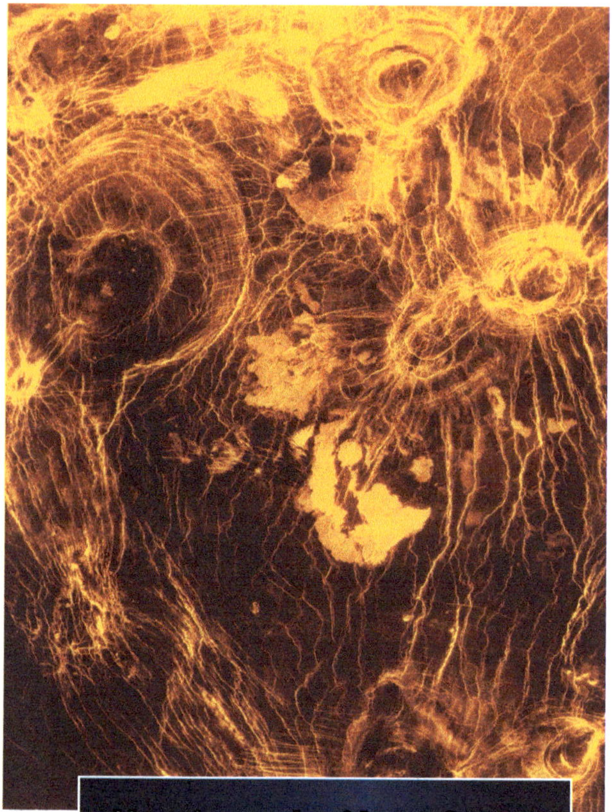

Venusian arachnoid, a surface feature of unknown origin.

resentative of all locations on the planet. Radar data from the U.S. Magellan spacecraft, which studied Venus from orbit in the early 1990s, provided global information about the roughness of the Venusian surface at scales of metres to tens of metres. Although much of the planet is indeed covered by lowland plains that appear smooth to radar, some terrains were found to be very much rougher. These include areas covered by ejecta (the material expelled from impact craters and extending around them), steep slopes associated with tectonic activity, and some lava flows. How such terrains would appear from a lander's perspective is not known, but large boulders and other sorts of angular blocks presumably would be more common than at the Venera sites.

## VENUS'S SURFACE COMPOSITION

A number of the Soviet landers carried instruments to analyze the chemical composition of the surface materials of Venus. The Venera 8 site gave indications that the rock composition may be similar to that of granite or other igneous rocks that compose Earth's continents. This inference, however, was based only on rather uncertain measurements of the concentrations of a few radioactive elements. Measurements of radioactive elements at the Venera 9 and 10 and Vega 1 and 2 landing sites suggested that the compositions there resemble those of basalt rocks found on Earth's ocean floors and in some volcanic regions such as Hawaii and Iceland. The Venera 13 and 14 and Vega 2 X-ray instruments measured concentrations of silicon, aluminum, magnesium, iron, calcium, potassium, titanium, manganese, and sulfur. Although some differences in composition were seen among the three sites, on the whole the elemental compositions measured by all three landers were similar to those of basalts on Earth.

A surprising result of orbital radar observations of Venus is that the highest elevations on the planet exhibit anomalously high radar reflectivity. The best interpretation seems to be that the highest elevations are coated with a thin layer of some semiconducting material. Its composition is unknown, but it could be an iron-containing mineral such as pyrite or magnetite, which formed at cooler, higher elevations from low concentrations of atmospheric iron(II) chloride vapour in the atmosphere.

## SURFACE FEATURES

Earth-based observatories and Venus-orbiting spacecraft have provided global-scale information on the nature of the planet's surface. All have used radar systems to penetrate the thick Venusian clouds.

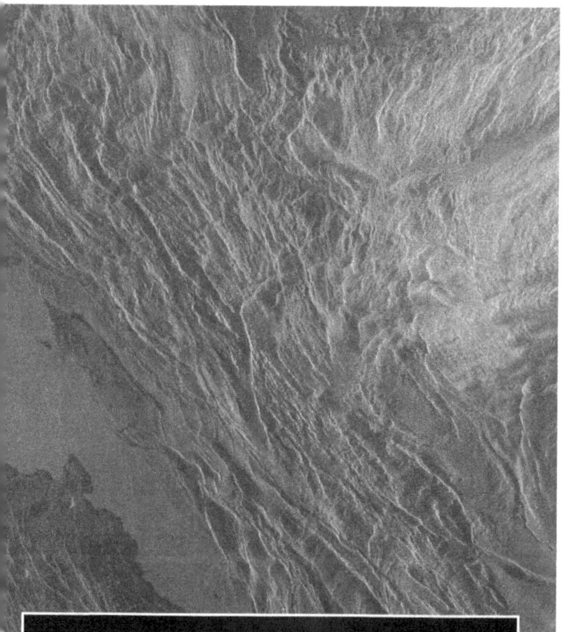

Akna Montes, a mountain belt on Venus.

The entire surface of the planet is dry and rocky. Because there is no sea level in the literal sense, elevation is commonly expressed as a planetary radius—i.e., as the distance from the centre of the planet to the surface at a given location. Another method, in which elevation is expressed as the distance above or below the planet's mean radius, is also used. Most of the planet consists of gently rolling plains. In some areas the elevations change by only a few hundred metres over distances of hundreds of kilometres. Globally, more than 80 percent of the surface deviates less than 1 km (0.6 mile) from the mean radius. At several locations on the plains are broad, gently sloping topographic depressions, or lowlands, that may reach several thousand kilometres across; they include Atalanta Planitia, Guinevere Planitia, and Lavinia Planitia. (Most features on Venus are named after mythological goddesses, legendary heroines, famous women from history, and names for Venus itself in different languages.)

Two striking features are the continent-sized highland areas, or terrae—Ishtar Terra in the northern hemisphere and Aphrodite Terra along the equator. Ishtar is roughly the size of Australia, while Aphrodite is comparable in area to South America.

Ishtar possesses the most spectacular topography on Venus. Much of its interior is a high plateau, called Lakshmi Planum, that resembles in configuration the Plateau of Tibet on Earth. Lakshmi is bounded by mountains on most sides, the largest range being the enormous Maxwell Montes on the east. These mountains soar about 11 km (7 miles) above the mean radius of Venus. The topography of Aphrodite, more complex than that of Ishtar, is characterized by a number of distinct mountain ranges and several deep, narrow troughs. In addition to the two main terrae are several smaller elevated regions, including Alpha Regio, Beta Regio, and Phoebe Regio.

Many of the surface features on Venus can be attributed to tectonic activity—that is, to deformational motions within the crust. These include mountain belts, plains deformation belts, rifts, coronae, and tesserae.

## MOUNTAIN BELTS OF VENUS

Found in the terrae, Venus's mountain belts are in some ways similar to ones on Earth such as the Himalayas of Asia and the Andes of South America. Among the best examples are those that encircle Lakshmi Planum, which in addition to Maxwell Montes include Freyja, Akna, and Danu Montes. Maxwell Montes is particularly broad and comparable in size to the Himalayas.

Venus's mountain belts typically consist of parallel ridges and troughs with spacings of 5–10 km (3–6 miles). They probably developed when broad bands of the lithosphere were compressed from the sides and became thickened, folding and thrusting surface materials upward. Their formation in some respects thus resembles the building of many mountain ranges on Earth. On the other hand, because of the lack of liquid water or ice on Venus, their appearance differs in major ways from their counterparts on Earth. Without the flow of rivers or glaciers to wear

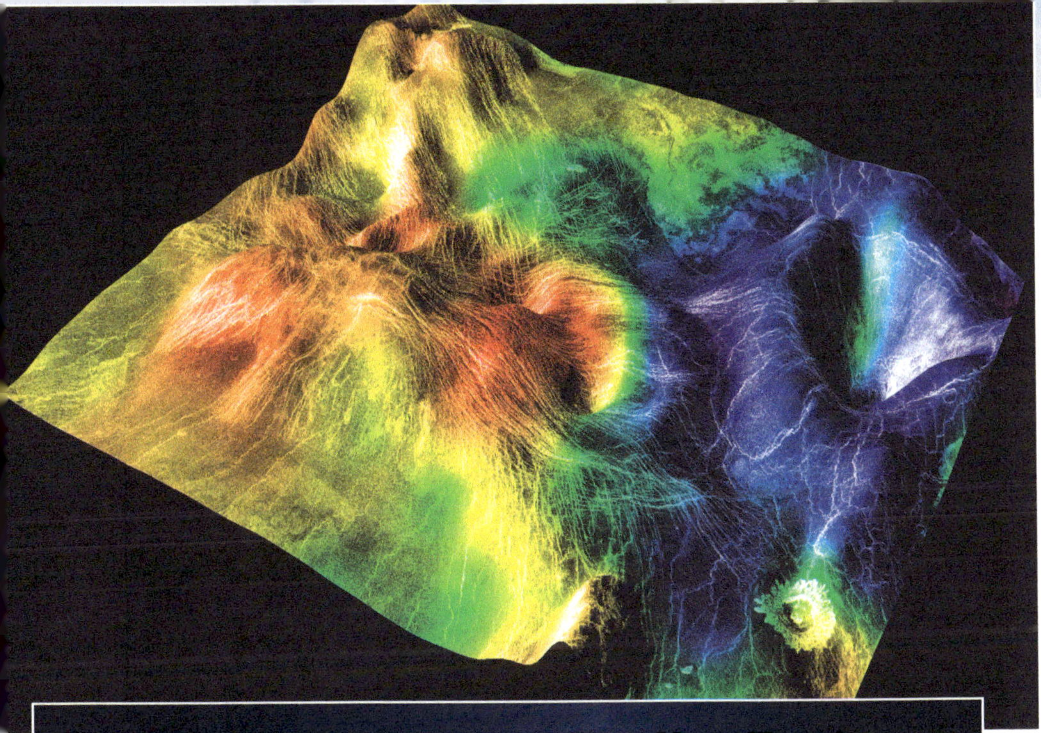

Vertically exaggerated view of a rift valley on Venus. The colours represent the degree of natural radio and infrared emission of the surface materials, which provide clues about their composition.

them down, Venusian mountain belts have acquired steep slopes as a result of folding and faulting. In some places the slopes have become so steep that they have collapsed under their own weight. The erosional forms common in mountainous regions on Earth are absent.

## RIFTS

Rifts are among the most spectacular tectonic features on Venus. The best-developed rifts are found atop broad, raised areas such as Beta Regio, sometimes radiating outward from their centres like the spokes of a giant wheel.

Beta and several other similar regions on Venus appear to be places where large areas of the lithosphere have been forced upward from below, splitting the surface to form great rift valleys.

The rifts are composed of innumerable faults, and their floors typically lie 1–2 km (0.6–1.2 miles) below the surrounding terrain. In many ways the rifts on Venus are similar to great rifts elsewhere, such as the East African Rift on Earth or Valles Marineris on Mars; volcanic eruptions, for example, appear to have been associated with all these features. The Venusian rifts differ from Earth and Martian ones, however, in that little erosion has taken place within them owing to the lack of water.

## CORONAE

Coronae (Latin: "garlands" or "crowns") are landforms that apparently owe their origin to the effects of hot, buoyant blobs of material, known from terrestrial geology as diapirs, that originate deep beneath the surface of Venus. Coronae evolve through several stages. As diapirs first rise through the planet's interior and approach the surface, they can lift the rocks above them, fracturing the surface in a radial pattern. This results in a distinctive starburst of faults and fractures, often lying atop a broad, gently sloping topographic rise. (Such features are sometimes called novae, a name given to them when their evolutionary relationship to coronae was less certain.) Once a diapir has neared the surface and cooled, it loses its buoyancy. The initially raised crust then can sag under its own weight, developing concentric faults as it does so. The result is a circular-to-oval pattern of faults, fractures, and ridges. Volcanism can occur through all stages of corona formation. During the late stages it tends to obscure the radial faulting that is characteristic of the early stages.

Coronae are typically a few hundred kilometres in diameter. Although they may have a raised outer rim, many coronae sag noticeably in their interiors and also outside their rims. Hundreds of coronae are found on Venus, observed at all stages of development. The radially fractured domes of the early stages are comparatively uncommon, while the concentric scars characteristic of mature coronae are among the most numerous large tectonic features on the planet.

## TESSERAE

Tesserae (Latin: "mosaic tiles") are the most geologically complex regions seen on Venus. Several large elevated regions, such as Alpha Regio, are composed largely of tessera terrain. Such terrain appears extraordinarily rugged and highly deformed in radar images, and in some instances it displays several different trends of parallel ridges and troughs that cut across one another at a wide range of angles. The deformation in tessera terrain can be so complex that sometimes it is difficult to determine what kinds of stresses in the lithosphere were responsible for forming it. In fact, probably no single process can explain all tessera formation. Tesserae typically appear very bright in radar images, which suggests an extremely rough and blocky surface at scales of metres. Some tesserae may be old terrain that has been subjected to more episodes of mountain building and faulting than have the materials around it, each one superimposed on its predecessor to produce the complex pattern observed.

## IMPACT CRATERS

The Venusian surface has been altered by objects from outside the planet as well as by forces from within. Impact craters dot the landscape, created by meteorites that passed through the atmosphere and struck the surface.

Nearly all solid bodies in the solar system bear the scars of meteoritic impacts, with small craters typically being more common than large ones. This general tendency is encountered on Venus as well—craters a few hundred kilometres across are present but rare, while craters tens of kilometres in diameter and smaller are common.

Venus has an interesting limitation, however, in that craters smaller than about 1.5–2 km (1–1.2 miles) in diameter are not found. Their absence is attributable to the planet's dense atmosphere, which causes intense frictional heating and strong aerodynamic forces as meteorites plunge through it at high velocities. The larger meteorites reach the surface intact, but the smaller ones are slowed and fragmented in the atmosphere.

In fact, craters several kilometres in size—i.e., near the minimum size observed—tend not to be circular. Instead they have complex shapes, often with several irregular pits rather than a single central depression, which suggests that the impacting body broke up into a number of fragments that struck the surface individually. Radar images also show diffuse dark and bright "smudges" that may be have resulted from the explosions of small meteorites above the surface.

For planets and moons that have impact craters, crater populations are an important source of information about the ages of the surfaces on which they lie. The concept is simple in principle—on a given body older surfaces have more craters than do younger ones. Determining an absolute age in years is difficult, however, and requires knowledge about the rate of crater formation, which usually must be inferred indirectly. The absolute ages of materials on the surface of Venus are not known, but the overall density of craters on Venus is lower than on many other bodies in the solar system. Estimates vary, but the average age of materials on Venus is almost certainly less than one billion years and may in fact be substantially less.

The spatial distribution of craters on Venus is essentially random. If craters were clustered in distinct regions, scientists could infer that a wide range of surface ages was represented over the planet. With a near-random global crater distribution, however, they are led instead to the conclusion that essentially the entire planet has been geologically resurfaced in the last billion years or less and that much of the resurfacing took place in a comparatively brief time.

## THE INTERIOR OF VENUS

Much less is known about the interior of Venus than about its surface and atmosphere. Nevertheless, because the planet is much like Earth in overall size and density and because it presumably accreted from similar materials, scientists expect that it evolved at least a crudely similar internal state. Therefore, it probably has a core of metal, a mantle of dense rock, and a crust of less-dense rock. The core, like that of Earth, is probably composed primarily of iron and nickel, although Venus's somewhat lower density may indicate that its core also contains some other, less-dense material such as sulfur. Because no intrinsic magnetic field has been detected for Venus, there is no direct evidence for a metallic core, as there is for Earth. Calculations of Venus's internal structure suggest that the outer boundary of the core lies a little more than 3,000 km (1,860 miles) from the centre of the planet.

Above the core and below the crust lies Venus's mantle, making up the bulk of the planet's volume. Despite the high surface temperatures, temperatures within the mantle are likely similar to those in Earth's mantle. Even though a planetary mantle is composed of solid rock, the material there can slowly creep or flow, just as glacial ice does, allowing sweeping convective motions to take place. Convection is a great equalizer of the temperatures of planetary interiors. Similar to heat production within Earth, heat within Venus is thought to be generated by the decay of natural radioactive materials. This heat is transported to the surface by convection. If temperatures deep within Venus were substantially higher than those within Earth, the viscosity of the rocks in the mantle would drop sharply, speeding convection and removing the heat more rapidly. Therefore, the deep interiors of Venus and Earth are not expected to differ dramatically in temperature.

As noted, the composition of the Venusian crust is believed to be dominated by basalt. Gravity data suggest that the thickness of the crust is fairly uniform over much of the planet, with typical values of perhaps 20–50 km (12–30 miles). Possible exceptions are the tessera highlands,

## VENUS'S VOLCANOES

Along with intense tectonic activity, Venus has undergone much volcanism. The largest volcanic outpourings are the huge lava fields that cover most of the rolling plains. These are similar in many respects to fields of overlapping lava flows seen on other planets, including Earth, but they are far more extensive.

Individual flows are for the most part long and thin, which indicates that the erupting lavas were very fluid and hence were able to flow long distances over gentle slopes. Lavas on Earth and the Moon that flow this readily typically consist of basalts, and so it is probable that basalts are common on the plains of Venus as well.

Of the many types of lava-flow features seen on the Venusian plains, none are more remarkable than the long, sinuous canali. These meandering channels usually have remarkably constant widths, which can be as much as 3 km (2 miles). They commonly extend as far as 500 km (300 miles) across the surface; one is 6,800 km (4,200 miles) long.

Other channel-like volcanic features on Venus include sinuous rilles that may be collapsed lava tubes, and large, complex compound valleys that apparently result from particularly massive outpourings of lava.

The volcano Sifs Mons. Lava flows having rougher surfaces appear brighter than smoother flows and are therefore presumably more recent.

In many locations on Venus, volcanic eruptions have built edifices similar to the great volcanoes of Hawaii on Earth or those associated with the Tharsis region on Mars. Sif Mons is an example of such a volcano; there are more than 100 others distributed widely over the planet. Known as shield volcanoes, they reach heights of several kilometres above the surrounding plains and can be hundreds of kilometres across at their base. They are made up of many individual lava flows piled on one another in a radial pattern.

(CONTINUED ON THE NEXT PAGE)

(CONTINUED FROM THE PREVIOUS PAGE)

Along with the extensive lava plains and the massive shield volcanoes are many smaller volcanic landforms. Enormous numbers of small volcanic cones are distributed throughout the plains. Particularly unusual in appearance are so-called pancake domes, which are typically a few tens of kilometres in diameter and about 1 km (0.6 mile) high and are remarkably circular in shape. Flat-topped and steep-sided, they appear to have formed when a mass of thick lava was extruded from a central vent and spread outward for a short distance in all directions before solidifying.

The Venus Express spacecraft found evidence for active volcanoes on Venus. A sharp rise in the amount of sulfur dioxide in the atmosphere in 2006 could have been from volcanic eruptions. In 2008 a hot spot was observed coming into existence and then cooling down again in the Ganiki Chasma rift zone.

where the crust may be significantly thicker.

Despite the many overall similarities between Venus and Earth, the geologic evolution of the two planets has been strikingly different. Evidence suggests that the process of plate tectonics does not now operate on Venus.

A trio of impact craters in a lowland plain in the southern hemisphere of Venus. The craters' surrounding ejecta blankets stand out as bright (and hence comparatively rough) terrain.

Although deformation of the lithosphere does indeed seem to be driven by mantle motions, lithospheric plates do not move mainly horizontally relative to each other, as they do on Earth. Instead, motions are mostly vertical, with the lithosphere warping up and down in response to the underlying convective motions. Volcanism, coronae, and rifts tend to be concentrated in regions of upwelling, while plains deformation belts are concentrated in regions of downwelling. The formation of rugged uplands such as Aphrodite and Ishtar is not as well understood, but the mechanism probably involves some kind of local crustal thickening in response to mantle motions.

The lack of plate tectonics on Venus may be due in part to the planet's high surface temperature, which makes the upper rigid layer of the planet—the lithosphere—more buoyant and hence more resistant to subduction than Earth's lithosphere, other factors being equal. Interestingly, there is evidence that the Venusian lithosphere may be thicker than Earth's and that it has thickened with time. A gradual, long-term thickening of Venus's lithosphere in fact could be related to the curious conclusion drawn from Venus's cratering record—that most of the planet underwent a brief but intense period of geologic resurfacing less than a billion years ago. One possible explanation is that Venus may experience episodic global overturns of its mantle, in which an initially thin lithosphere slowly thickens until it founders on a near-global scale, triggering a brief, massive geologic resurfacing event. How many times this may have occurred during the planet's history and when it may happen again are unknown.

CHAPTER 3

# EARTH

The third planet from the Sun is Earth, the home of all known life. While it shares many characteristics with other inner planets, its physical properties and history allow it to support life in its near-surface environment. In fact, life itself has greatly altered the planet in ways that generally help maintain the conditions for life. Scientists have come to view Earth as a dynamic world with many interacting systems. Understanding these relationships will surely be important as human activities increasingly affect the planet's surface, oceans, and atmosphere.

Scientists have applied the full battery of modern instrumentation to studying Earth in ways that have not yet been possible for the other planets; thus, much more is known about its structure and composition. This detailed knowledge, in turn, provides deeper insight into the mechanisms by which planets in general cool down, by which their magnetic fields are generated, and by which the separation of lighter elements from heavier ones as planets

A composite image of Earth captured by instruments aboard NASA's Suomi National Polar-orbiting Partnership satellite, 2012.

develop their internal structure releases additional energy for geologic processes and alters crustal compositions.

The mean distance of Earth from the Sun is about 149,600,000 km (92,960,000 miles). The planet orbits the Sun in a path that is presently more nearly a circle (less eccentric) than are the orbits of all but two of the other planets, Venus and Neptune. Earth makes one revolution, or one complete orbit of the Sun, in about 365.25 days. The direction of revolution—counterclockwise as viewed down from the north—is in the same sense, or direction, as the rotation of the Sun; Earth's spin, or rotation about its axis, is also in the same sense, which is called direct or prograde.

The rotation period, or length of a sidereal day—23 hours, 56 minutes, and 4 seconds—is similar to that of Mars. Jupiter and most asteroids have days less than half as long, while Mercury and Venus have days more nearly comparable to their orbital periods. The 23.44° tilt, or inclination, of Earth's axis to its orbital plane, also typical, results in greater heating and more hours of daylight in one hemisphere or the other over the course of a year and so is responsible for the cyclic change of seasons.

With an equatorial radius of 6,378 km (3,963 miles), Earth is the largest of the four inner planets, but it is considerably smaller than the gas giants of the outer solar system. Earth has a single natural satellite, the Moon, which orbits the planet at a mean distance of about 384,400 km (238,900 miles). The Moon is one of the bigger natural satellites in the solar system; only the giant planets have moons comparable or larger in size. Some planetary astronomers consider the Earth-Moon system a double planet, with some similarity in that regard to the dwarf planet Pluto and its largest moon, Charon.

Earth's gravitational field is manifested as the attractive force acting on a free body at rest, causing it to accelerate in the general direction of the centre of the planet. Departures from the spherical shape and the effect of Earth's rotation cause gravity to vary with latitude over the terrestrial surface. The average gravitational acceleration at sea level is about 980 cm/sec$^2$ (32.2 feet/sec$^2$).

Earth's gravity keeps the Moon in its orbit around the planet and also generates tides in the solid body of the Moon. Such deformations are manifested in the form of slight bulges at the lunar surface, detectable only by sensitive instruments. In turn, the Moon's mass—relatively large for a natural satellite—exerts a gravitational force that causes tides on Earth. The Sun, much more distant but vastly more massive, also raises tides on Earth.

The tides are most apparent as the twice-daily and daily rises and falls of the ocean water, although tidal deformations occur in the solid Earth and in the atmosphere as well. The movement of the water throughout the ocean basins as a result of the tides (as well as, to a lesser extent, the tidal distortion of the solid Earth) dissipates orbital kinetic energy as heat, producing a gradual slowing of Earth's rotation and a spiraling outward of the Moon's orbit. Currently this slowing lengthens the day by a few thousandths of a second per century, but the rate of slowing varies with time as plate tectonics and sea-level changes alter the areas covered by inland bays and shallow seas.

The blankets of volatile gases and liquids near and above the surface of Earth are, along with solar energy, of prime importance to the sustenance of life on Earth. They are distributed and recycled throughout the atmosphere and hydrosphere of the planet.

## EARTH'S ATMOSPHERE

Earth is surrounded by a relatively thin atmosphere consisting of a mixture of gases, primarily molecular nitrogen (78 percent) and molecular oxygen (21 percent). Also present are much smaller amounts of gases such as argon (nearly 1 percent), water vapour (averaging 1 percent but highly variable in time and location), carbon dioxide (0.0395 percent [395 parts per million] and presently rising), methane (0.00018 percent [1.8 parts per million] and presently rising), and others, along with minute solid and liquid particles in suspension.

Because Earth has a weak gravitational field (by virtue of its size) and warm atmospheric temperatures (due to its proximity to the Sun) compared with the giant planets, it lacks the most common gases in the universe that they possess: hydrogen and helium. Whereas both the Sun and Jupiter are composed predominantly of these two elements, they could not be retained long on early Earth and rapidly evaporated into interplanetary space.

The high oxygen content of Earth's atmosphere is out of the ordinary. Oxygen is a highly reactive gas that, under most planetary conditions, would be combined with other chemicals in the atmosphere, surface, and crust. It is in fact supplied continuously by biological processes; without life, there would be virtually no free oxygen. The

Planet Earth rising above the lunar horizon, an unprecedented view captured in December 1968 from the Apollo 8 spacecraft as its orbit carried it clear of the far side of the Moon.

1.8 parts per million of methane in the atmosphere is also far out of chemical equilibrium with the atmosphere and crust: it, too, is of biological origin, with the contribution by human activities far outweighing others.

The gases of the atmosphere extend from the surface of Earth to heights of thousands of kilometres, eventually merging with the solar wind—a stream of charged particles that flows outward from the outermost regions of the Sun. The composition of the atmosphere is more or less constant with height to an altitude of about 100 km (60 miles), with particular exceptions being water vapour and ozone.

The atmosphere is commonly described in terms of distinct layers, or regions. Most of the atmosphere is concentrated in the troposphere, which extends from the surface to an altitude of about 10–15 km (6–9 miles), depending on latitude and season. The behaviour of the gases in this layer is controlled by convection. This process involves the turbulent, overturning motions resulting from buoyancy of near-surface air that is warmed by the Sun. Convection maintains a decreasing vertical temperature gradient—i.e., a temperature decline with altitude—of roughly 6 °C (10.8 °F) per km through the troposphere. At the top of the troposphere, which is called the tropopause, temperatures have fallen to about −80 °C (−112 °F). The troposphere is the region where nearly all water vapour exists and essentially all weather occurs.

The dry, tenuous stratosphere lies above the troposphere and extends to an altitude of about 50 km (30 miles). Convective motions are weak or absent in the stratosphere; motions instead tend to be horizontally oriented. The temperature in this layer increases with altitude.

In the upper stratospheric regions, absorption of ultraviolet light from the Sun breaks down molecular oxygen ($O_2$); recombination of single oxygen atoms with $O_2$ molecules into ozone ($O_3$) creates the shielding ozone layer.

Above the relatively warm stratopause is the even more tenuous mesosphere, in which temperatures again decline with altitude to 80–90 km (50–56 miles) above the surface, where the mesopause is defined. The minimum temperature attained there is extremely variable with season. Temperatures then rise with increasing height through the overlying layer known as the thermosphere. Also above about 80–90 km there is an increasing fraction of charged, or ionized, particles, which from this altitude upward defines the ionosphere. Spectacular visible auroras are generated in this region, particularly along approximately circular zones around the poles, by the interaction of nitrogen and oxygen atoms in the atmosphere with episodic bursts of energetic particles originating from the Sun.

Earth's general atmospheric circulation is driven by the energy of sunlight, which is more abundant in equatorial latitudes. Movement of this heat toward the poles is strongly affected by Earth's rapid rotation and the associated Coriolis force at latitudes away from the Equator (which adds an east-west component to the direction of the winds), resulting in multiple cells of circulating air in each hemisphere.

Instabilities (perturbations in the atmospheric flow that grow with time) produce the characteristic high-pressure areas and low-pressure storms of the midlatitudes as well as the fast, eastward-moving jet streams of the upper troposphere that guide the paths of storms. The oceans are massive reservoirs of heat that act largely to smooth out variations in Earth's global temperatures, but their slowly changing currents and temperatures also influence weather and climate, as in the El Niño/Southern Oscillation weather phenomenon.

Earth's atmosphere is not a static feature of the environment. Rather, its composition has evolved over geologic time in concert with life and is changing more rapidly today in response to human activities. Roughly halfway through the history of Earth, the atmosphere's unusually high abundance of free oxygen began to develop, through photosynthesis by cyanobacteria and saturation of natural surface sinks of oxygen (e.g., relatively oxygen-poor minerals and hydrogen-rich gases exuded from volcanoes). Accumulation of oxygen made it possible for complex cells, which consume oxygen during metabolism and of which all plants and animals are composed, to develop.

The physics of hydrogen fusion leads astronomers to conclude that the Sun was 30 percent less luminous during the earliest history of Earth than it is today. Hence, all else being equal, the oceans should have been frozen. Observations of Earth's planetary neighbours, Mars and Venus, and estimates of the carbon locked in Earth's crust at present suggest that there was much more carbon dioxide in Earth's atmosphere during earlier periods. This would have enhanced warming of the surface via the greenhouse effect and so allowed the oceans to remain liquid.

Today there is 100,000 times more carbon dioxide buried in carbonate rocks in Earth's crust than in the atmosphere, in sharp contrast to Venus, whose atmospheric evolution followed a different course. On Earth, the formation of carbonate shells by marine life is the principal mechanism for transforming carbon dioxide to carbonates; abiotic processes involving liquid water also produce carbonates, albeit more slowly. On Venus, however, life never had the chance to arise and to generate carbonates. Because of the planet's location in the solar system, early Venus received 10–20 percent more sunlight than falls on Earth even today, despite the fainter young Sun at the time.

Most planetary scientists believe that the elevated surface temperature that resulted kept water from condensing to a liquid. Instead, it remained in the atmosphere as water vapour, which, like carbon dioxide, is an efficient greenhouse gas. Together the two gases caused surface temperatures to rise even higher so that massive amounts of water escaped to the stratosphere, where it was dissociated by solar ultraviolet radiation. With conditions now too hot and dry to permit abiotic carbonate formation, most or all of the planet's inventory of carbon remained in the atmosphere as carbon dioxide. Models predict that Earth may suffer the same fate in a billion years, when the Sun exceeds its present brightness by 10–20 percent.

Between the late 1950s and the end of the 20th century, the amount of carbon dioxide in Earth's atmosphere increased by more than 15 percent because of the burning of fossil fuels (e.g., coal, oil, and natural gas) and the destruction of tropical rainforests, such as that of the

Amazon River basin. Computer models predict that a net doubling of carbon dioxide by the middle of the 21st century could lead to a global warming of 1.5–4.5 °C (2.7–8.1 °F) averaged over the planet, which would have profound effects on sea level and agriculture. Although this conclusion has been criticized by some on the basis that the warming observed so far has not kept pace with the projection, analyses of ocean temperature data have suggested that much of the warming during the 20th century actually occurred in the oceans themselves—and will eventually appear in the atmosphere.

Another present concern regarding the atmosphere is the impact of human activities on the stratospheric ozone layer. Complex chemical reactions involving traces of man-made chlorofluorocarbons (CFCs) were found in the mid-1980s to be creating temporary holes in the ozone layer, particularly over Antarctica, during polar spring. Yet more disturbing was the discovery of a growing depletion of ozone over the highly populated temperate latitudes, since the short-wavelength ultraviolet radiation that the ozone layer effectively absorbs has been found to cause skin cancer. International agreements in place to halt the production of the most egregious ozone-destroying CFCs will eventually halt and reverse the depletion, but only by the middle of the 21st century, because of the long residence time of these chemicals in the stratosphere.

## EARTH'S HYDROSPHERE

Earth's hydrosphere is a discontinuous layer of water at or near the planet's surface; it includes all liquid and frozen surface waters, groundwater held in soil and rock, and atmospheric water vapour. Unique within the solar system, the hydrosphere is essential to all life as it is presently understood. Earth has a surface area of roughly 510,066,000 square km (196,938,000 square miles); almost 71 percent of Earth's surface is covered by saltwater oceans, with a volume of about 1.4 billion cubic km (336 million

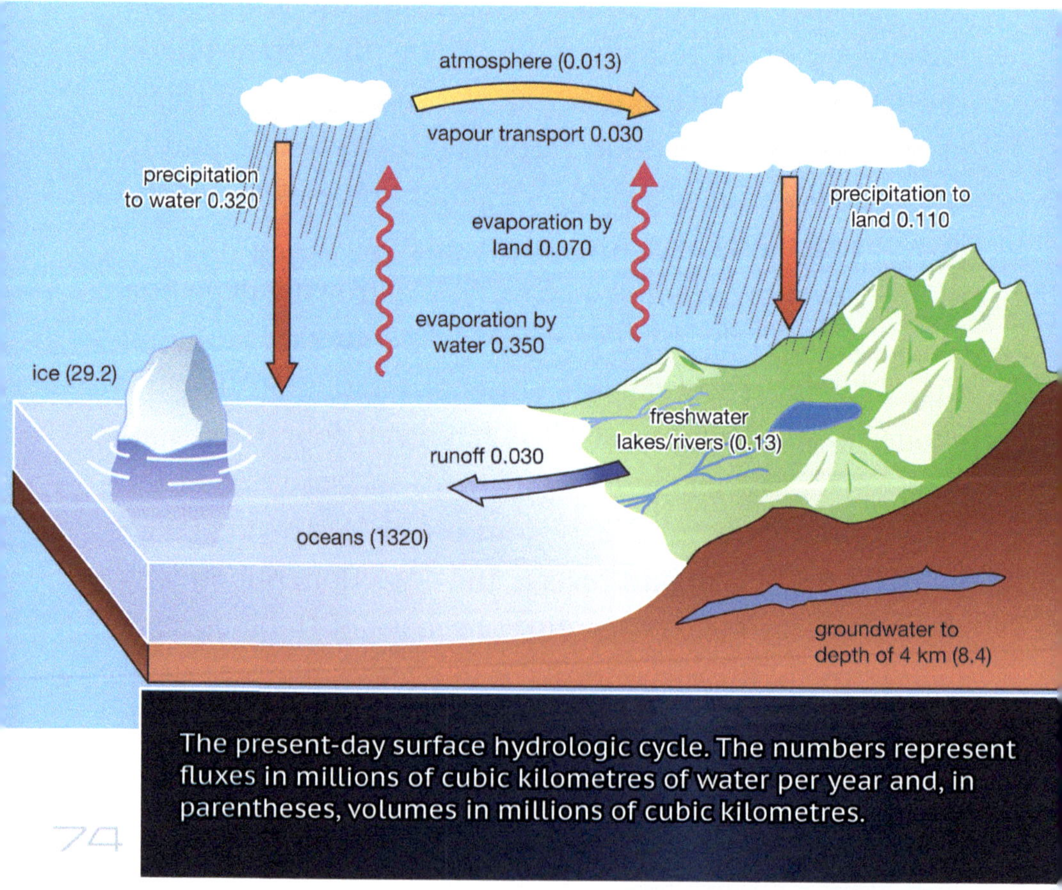


The present-day surface hydrologic cycle. The numbers represent fluxes in millions of cubic kilometres of water per year and, in parentheses, volumes in millions of cubic kilometres.

cubic miles) and an average temperature of about 4 °C (39.2 °F), not far above the freezing point of water. The oceans contain about 97 percent of the planet's water volume. The remainder occurs as fresh water, three-quarters of which is locked up in the form of ice at polar latitudes. Most of the remaining fresh water is groundwater held in soils and rocks; less than 1 percent of it occurs in lakes and rivers. In terms of percentage, atmospheric water vapour is negligible, but the transport of water evaporated from the oceans onto land surfaces is an integral part of the hydrologic cycle that renews and sustains life.

The hydrologic cycle involves the transfer of water from the oceans through the atmosphere to the continents and back to the oceans over and beneath the land surface. The cycle includes processes such as precipitation, evaporation, transpiration, infiltration, percolation, and runoff. These processes operate throughout the entire hydrosphere, which extends from about 15 km (9 miles) into the atmosphere to roughly 5 km (3 miles) into the crust.

About one-third of the solar energy that reaches Earth's surface is expended on evaporating ocean water. The resulting atmospheric moisture and humidity condense into clouds, rain, snow, and dew. Moisture is a crucial factor in determining weather. It is the driving force behind storms and is responsible for separating electrical charge, which is the cause of lightning and thus of natural wildland fires, which have an important role in some ecosystems. Moisture wets the land, replenishes subterranean aquifers, chemically weathers the rocks, erodes the landscape, nourishes life, and fills the rivers, which carry dissolved chemicals and sediments back into the oceans.

Water also plays a vital role in the carbon dioxide cycle (a part of the more inclusive carbon cycle). Under the action of water and dissolved carbon dioxide, calcium is weathered from continental rocks and carried to the oceans, where it combines to form calcium carbonates (including shells of marine life). Eventually the carbonates are deposited on the seafloor and are lithified to form limestones. Some of these carbonate rocks are later dragged deep into Earth's interior by the global process of plate tectonics and melted, resulting in a rerelease of carbon dioxide (from volcanoes, for example) into the atmosphere.

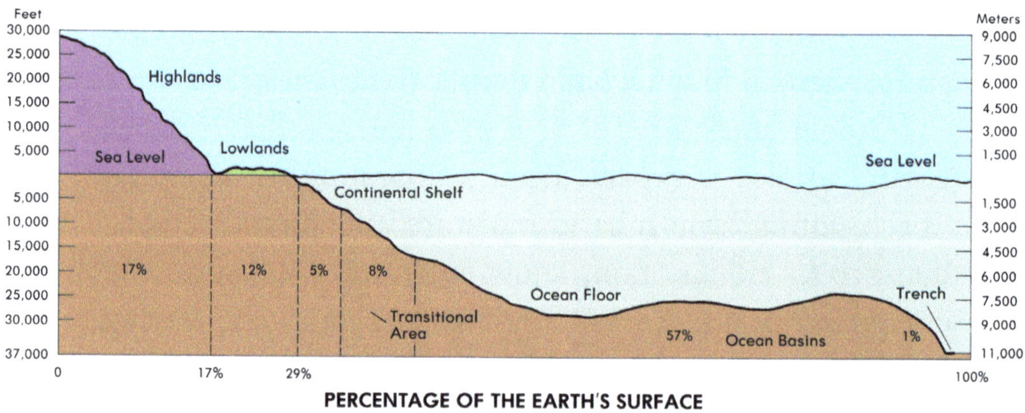


Percentage of Earth's surface devoted to various land and water features.

Cyclic processing of water, carbon dioxide, and oxygen through geologic and biological systems on Earth has been fundamental to maintaining the habitability of the planet with time and to shaping the erosion and weathering of the continents, and it contrasts sharply with the lack of such processes on Venus. (Evidence of past episodes of liquid water erosion—and possibly limited amounts of such erosion today—has been found on Mars.)

## EARTH'S OUTER SHELL

Earth's outermost, rigid, rocky layer is called the crust. It is composed of low-density, easily melted rocks; the continental crust is predominantly granitic rock, while composition of the oceanic crust corresponds mainly to that of basalt and gabbro. Analyses of seismic waves, generated by earthquakes within Earth's interior, show that the crust extends about 50 km (30 miles) beneath the continents but only 5–10 km (3–6 miles) beneath the ocean floors.

At the base of the crust, a sharp change in the observed behaviour of seismic waves marks the interface with the mantle. The mantle is composed of denser rocks, on which the rocks of the crust float. On geologic timescales, the mantle behaves as a very viscous fluid and responds to stress by flowing. Together the uppermost mantle and the crust act mechanically as a single rigid layer, called the lithosphere.

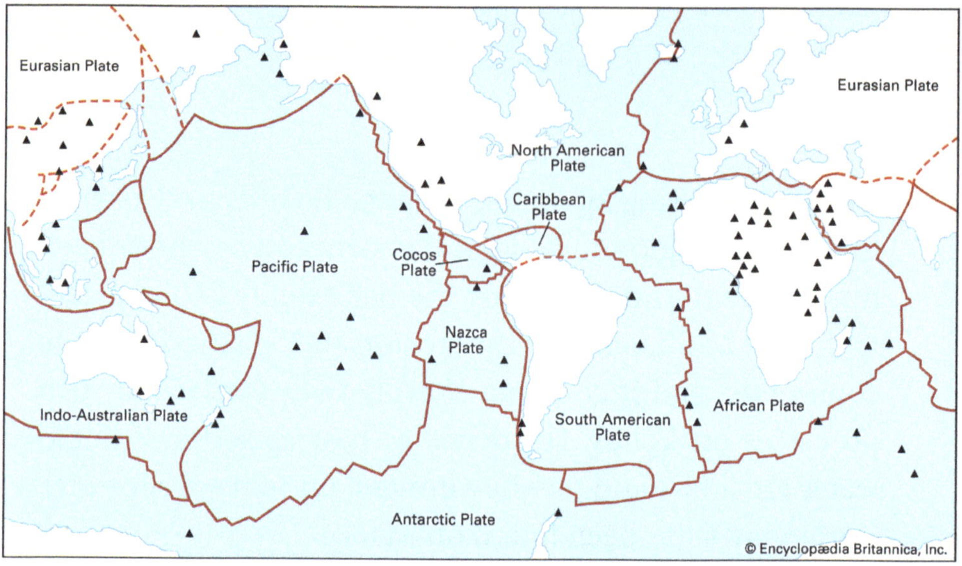


The principal tectonic plates that make up Earth's lithosphere. Also located are several dozen hot spots, indicated by triangles, where plumes of hot mantle material are upwelling beneath the plates.

The lithospheric outer shell of Earth is not one continuous piece but is broken, like a slightly cracked eggshell, into about a dozen major separate rigid blocks, or plates. There are two types of plates, oceanic and continental. An example of an oceanic plate is the Pacific Plate, which extends from the East Pacific Rise to the deep-sea trenches bordering the western part of the Pacific basin. A continental plate is exemplified by the North American Plate, which includes North America as well as the oceanic crust between it and a portion of the Mid-Atlantic Ridge. The latter is an enormous submarine mountain chain that extends down the axis of the Atlantic basin, passing midway between Africa and North and South America.

The lithospheric plates are about 60 km (35 miles) thick beneath the oceans and 100–200 km (60–120 miles) beneath the continents. (It should be noted that these thicknesses are defined by the mechanical rigidity of the lithospheric material. They do not correspond to the thickness of the crust, which is defined at its base by the discontinuity in seismic wave behaviour, as cited above.) They ride on a weak, perhaps partially molten, layer of the upper mantle called the asthenosphere. Slow convection currents deep within the mantle generated by radioactive heating of the interior drive lateral movements of the plates (and the continents on top of them) at a rate of several centimetres per year. The plates interact along their margins, and these boundaries are classified into three general types on the basis of the relative motions of the adjacent plates: divergent, convergent, and transform (or strike-slip).

## THE INTERIOR OF EARTH

More than 90 percent of Earth's mass is composed of iron, oxygen, silicon, and magnesium, elements that can form the crystalline minerals known as silicates. Nevertheless, in chemical and mineralogical composition, as in physical properties, Earth is far from homogeneous. Apart from the superficial lateral differences near the surface (i.e., in the compositions of the continental and oceanic crusts), Earth's principal differences vary with distance toward the centre. This is due to increasing temperatures and pressures and to the original segregation of materials, soon after Earth accreted from the solar nebula about 4.56 billion years ago, into a metal-rich core, a silicate-rich mantle, and the more highly refined crustal rocks. Earth is geochemically differentiated to a great extent. Crustal rocks contain several times as much of the rock-forming element aluminum as does the rest of the solid Earth and many dozens of times as much uranium. On the other hand, the crust, which accounts for a mere 0.4 percent of Earth's mass, contains less than 0.1 percent of its iron. Between 85 and 90 percent of Earth's iron is concentrated in the core.

With a radius of almost 3,500 km (2,200 miles), Earth's core is about the size of the entire planet Mars. About one-third of Earth's mass is contained in the core, most of which is liquid iron alloyed with nickel and some lighter, cosmically abundant components (e.g., sulfur, oxygen, and, controversially, even hydrogen). Its liquid nature is revealed by the failure of shear-type seismic waves to penetrate the core.

A small, central part of the core, however, below a depth of about 5,100 km (3,200 miles), is solid iron. This inner core is itself divided into two layers known only by the polarity differences of the iron crystals found within them. The polarity of the iron crystals of the innermost

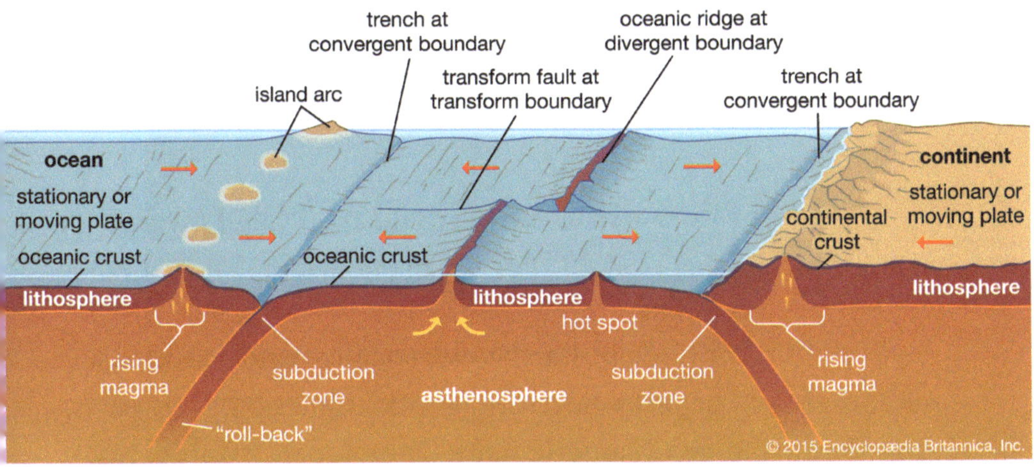


Production and destruction of Earth's crust according to the theory of plate tectonics.

layer is oriented in an east-west direction, whereas that of the outermost layer is oriented north-south.

Temperatures in the core are extremely hot, ranging from 4,000–5,000 K (roughly 6,700–8,500 °F; 3,700–4,700 °C) at the outer part of the core to 5,000–7,000 K (8,500–12,100 °F; 4,700–6,700 °C) in the centre, comparable to the surface of the Sun. Large uncertainties in temperature arise from questions as to which compounds form alloys with iron in the core, and more recent data favour the lower end of the temperature estimates for the inner core. The core's reservoir of heat may contribute as much as one-fifth of all the internal heat that ultimately flows to the surface of Earth. The basic structure of Earth—crust, mantle, and core—appears to be replicated on the other terrestrial planets, though with substantial variations in the relative size of each region.

## EARTH'S GEOMAGNETIC FIELD AND MAGNETOSPHERE

Helical fluid motions in Earth's electrically conducting liquid outer core have an electromagnetic dynamo effect, giving rise to the geomagnetic field. The planet's sizable, hot core, along with its rapid spin, probably accounts for the exceptional strength of the magnetic field of Earth compared with those of the other terrestrial planets. Venus, for example, which has a metallic core that may be similar to Earth's in size, rotates very slowly and has no detected intrinsic magnetic field. Mercury and Mars have only small intrinsic magnetic fields.

Earth's main magnetic field permeates the planet and an enormous volume of space surrounding it. A great teardrop-shaped region of space called the magnetosphere is formed by the interaction of Earth's field with the solar wind. At a distance of about 65,000 km (40,000 miles) outward toward the Sun, the pressure of the solar wind is balanced by the geomagnetic field. This serves as an obstacle to the solar wind, and the flow of charged particles, or plasma, is deflected around Earth by the resulting bow shock. The magnetosphere so produced streams out into an elongated magnetotail that stretches several million kilometres downstream from Earth away from the Sun.

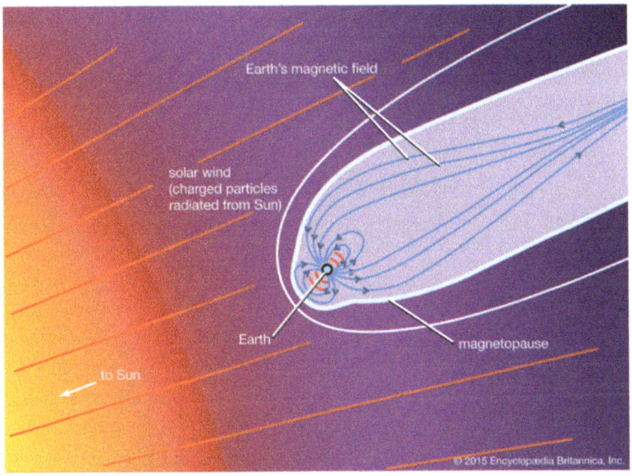


Earth's magnetosphere. The magnetosphere's tail is created by the solar wind.

Plasma particles from the solar wind can leak through the magnetopause, the sunward boundary of the magnetosphere, and populate its interior; charged particles from the Earth's ionosphere also enter the magnetosphere. The magnetotail can store for hours an enormous amount of energy—several billion megajoules, which is roughly equivalent to the yearly electricity production of many smaller countries. This occurs through a process called reconnection, in which the Sun's magnetic field, dragged into interplanetary space by the solar wind, becomes linked with the magnetic field in Earth's magnetosphere. The energy is released in dynamic structural reconfigurations of the magnetosphere, called geomagnetic substorms, which often result in the precipitation of energetic particles into the ionosphere, giving rise to fluorescing auroral displays.

Converging magnetic field lines fairly close to Earth can trap highly energetic particles so that they gyrate between the Northern and Southern hemispheres and slowly drift longitudinally around the planet in two concentric doughnut-shaped zones known as the Van Allen radiation belts. Many of the charged particles trapped in these belts are produced when energetic cosmic rays strike Earth's upper atmosphere, producing neutrons that then decay into electrons, which are negatively charged, and protons, which are positively charged. Others come from the solar wind or Earth's atmosphere. The inner radiation belt was detected in 1958 by the American physicist James Van Allen and colleagues, using a Geiger-Müller counter aboard the first U.S. satellite, Explorer 1; the outer belt was distinguished by other U.S. and Soviet spacecraft launched the same year. Earth's magnetosphere has been extensively studied ever since, and space physicists have extended their studies of plasma processes to the vicinities of comets and other planets.

An important characteristic of Earth's magnetic field is polarity reversal. In this process the direction of the dipole component reverses—i.e., the north magnetic pole becomes the south magnetic pole and vice versa. From studying the direction of magnetization of many rocks, geologists know that such reversals occur, without a discernible pattern, at intervals that range from tens of thousands of years to millions of years, though they are still uncertain about the mechanisms responsible. It is likely that during the changeover, which is believed to take a few thousand years, a nondipolar field remains, at a small fraction of the strength of the normal field. In the temporary absence of the dipole component, the solar wind would approach much closer to Earth, allowing particles that are normally deflected by the field or are trapped in its outer portions to reach the surface. The increase in particle radiation could lead to increased rates of genetic damage and thus of mutations or sterility in plants and animals, leading to the disappearance of some species. Scientists have looked for evidence of such changes in the fossil record at times of past field reversals, but the results have been inconclusive.

## EARTH'S DEVELOPMENT

The most abundant elements in the Sun, hydrogen and helium, are severely lacking in the inner, terrestrial planets but are still abundant constituents of the large, gaseous, outer planets such as Jupiter and Saturn. It is thought that only at the distance of Jupiter and beyond—in the colder regions of the solar system, including the zone beyond Neptune in which comets originated—could the more volatile substances, which also include water, carbon dioxide, and ammonia, condense and be retained in appreciable amounts during the formation of the planets. Nevertheless, when the relative abundances of the less volatile

## IMPACTED BY PLANETESIMALS

During its accretion, Earth is thought to have been shock-heated by the impacts of meteorite-size bodies and larger planetesimals. For a meteorite collision, the heating is concentrated near the surface where the impact occurs, which allows the heat to radiate back into space. A planetesimal, however, can penetrate sufficiently deeply on impact to produce heating well beneath the surface. In addition, the debris formed on impact can blanket the planetary surface, which helps to retain heat inside the planet. Some scientists have suggested that, in this way, Earth may have become hot enough to begin melting after growing to less than 15 percent of its final volume.

Among the planetesimals striking the forming Earth, at least one is considered to have been comparable in size to Mars. Although the details are not well understood, there is good evidence that the impact of such a large planetesimal created the Moon. Among the more persuasive indications is that the relative abundances of many trace elements in rocks from the Moon are close to the values obtained for Earth's mantle. Unless this is a fortuitous coincidence, it points to the Moon having been derived from the mantle. Computer simulations have shown that a glancing collision of a Mars-size planetary body could have been sufficient to excavate from Earth's interior the material that would form the Moon. Again, the evidence for such large collisions suggests that Earth was very effectively heated during accretion.

It is apparent, then, that many processes contributing to the early development of Earth occurred almost simultaneously, within tens to hundreds of million of years after the Sun was formed. Meteorites and Earth were formed within this time, and the Moon, which has been dated at more than four billion years in age, apparently was formed in the same time period. Simultaneously, Earth's core was accumulating and may have been completely formed during the planet's growth period. In addition to the possible accretional heating caused by planetesimal impacts, the sinking of metal to form the core released enough gravitational energy to heat the entire planet by 1,000 K (1,800 °F; 1,000 °C) or more. Thus, once core formation began, Earth's interior became sufficiently hot to convect. Although it is not known whether or in what form plate tectonics was active at the surface, it seems quite possible that the underlying mantle convection began even before the planet had grown to its final dimensions. Only later in Earth's development did radioactivity become an important heat source as well.

elements are compared for the Sun, for a class of primitive, largely chemically unaltered meteorites called CI carbonaceous chondrites (considered by many researchers the most pristine samples of original solar system material), and for the estimated composition of Earth, their values are all in close agreement.

This is the basis for the chondritic model, which holds that Earth (and presumably the other terrestrial planets) was essentially built up from bodies made of such meteoritic material. This idea is corroborated by isotopic studies of rocks derived from interior regions of Earth considered to be little changed throughout the planet's history. Thus, it appears that the composition of Earth is roughly what would be expected given the observed elemental abundances in the Sun and accounting for the loss of the more volatile elements.

The dust and grains that condensed out of the cooling nebular gas aggregated gravitationally to form larger fragments of rock. The chondritic meteorites observed today are basically just such collections of grains and fragments that were compacted together into larger pieces. Through continued accretion, the smaller pieces formed boulders and asteroid-size bodies (planetesimals) and, ultimately, bodies the size of the Moon and Mars. The larger the planetesimals grew, the greater their gravitational attraction and the more effectively they swept up additional particles and rock fragments while circling the Sun. Growth slowed when most bodies were lunar- and Mars-size because they were limited in number and hence effectively isolated one from another in their orbits. As Jupiter increased to its giant size, its powerful gravity perturbed these "embryos" of the terrestrial planets, elongating their orbits and allowing their incremental growth to approximately the mass of Earth to proceed over tens of millions of years.

Stony meteorites and iron meteorites (those composed largely of iron alloyed with nickel and sulfur) both fall on Earth today, and both types are thought to have been present during the formation of the planetesimals that would accrete to become Earth. In other words, Earth seems to have accreted only after most, if not all, solid matter had already condensed. Thus, a wide range of minerals was included in the grains, the larger fragments, and even the planetesimals that were accumulated by the growing planet. Apparently, such an aggregation of dense metallic fragments and less dense rocky fragments is not very stable. Calculations based on the measured strengths of rocks indicate that the metallic fragments probably sank downward as Earth grew. Although the planet was relatively cold at this stage—less than 500 K (440 °F; 230 °C)—the rock was weak. This is an important point because it leads to the conclusion that Earth's metallic core began to form during accretion of the planet and probably before the planet had grown to one-fifth of its present volume.

CHAPTER 4

# MARS

The fourth planet from the Sun is Mars. Easily visible from Earth with the naked eye, it has intrigued stargazers since ancient times. It often appears quite bright and reddish in the night sky. Babylonians mentioned Mars in records from about 3,000 years ago, associating the blood-red planet with their god of death and disease. The name Mars is that of the ancient Roman god of war. As long as 3,000 years ago, Babylonian astronomer-astrologers called the planet Nergal for their god of death and pestilence. The planet's two moons, Phobos (Greek: "Fear") and Deimos ("Terror"), were named for two of the sons of Ares and Aphrodite (the counterparts of Mars and Venus, respectively, in Greek mythology).

In recent times Mars has intrigued people for more-substantial reasons than its baleful appearance. The planet is the second closest to Earth, after Venus, and it is usually easy to observe in the night sky because its orbit lies outside Earth's. It is also the only planet whose solid surface

A composite of images taken by the Mars Global Surveyor spacecraft showing an especially serene view of Mars. White water-ice clouds surround the most prominent volcanic peaks.

and atmospheric phenomena can be seen in telescopes from Earth.

Centuries of assiduous studies by earthbound observers, extended by spacecraft observations since the 1960s, have revealed that Mars is similar to Earth in many ways. Like Earth, Mars has clouds, winds, a roughly 24-hour day, seasonal weather patterns, polar ice caps, volcanoes, canyons, and other familiar features. There are intriguing clues that billions of years ago Mars was even more Earth-like than today, with a denser, warmer atmosphere and much more water—rivers, lakes, flood channels, and perhaps oceans.

By all indications Mars is now a sterile frozen desert, but close-up images of dark streaks on the slopes of some craters during Martian spring and summer suggest that at least small amounts of water may flow seasonally on the planet's surface and may still exist as a liquid in protected areas below the surface.

The presence of water on Mars is considered a critical issue because life as it is presently understood cannot exist without water. If microscopic life-forms ever did originate on Mars, there remains a chance, albeit a remote one, that they may yet survive in these hidden watery niches. In 1996 a team of scientists reported what they concluded to be evidence for ancient microbial life in a piece of meteorite that had come from Mars, but most scientists have disputed their interpretation.

## BASIC FEATURES OF MARS

Mars is the fourth planet out from the Sun. It moves around the Sun at a mean distance of 228 million km (140 million miles), or about 1.5 times the distance of Earth from the Sun. Because of Mars's relatively elongated orbit, the distance between Mars and the Sun varies from 206.6 million to 249.2 million km (128.4 million to 154.8 million miles). Mars orbits the Sun once in 687 Earth days, which means that its year is nearly twice as long as Earth's. At its closest approach, Mars is less than 56 million km (35 million miles) from Earth, but it recedes to almost 400 million km (250 million miles) when the two planets are on opposite sides of the solar system.

Mars is easiest to observe when it and the Sun are in opposite directions in the sky—i.e., at opposition—because it is then high in the sky and shows a fully lighted face. Successive oppositions occur about every 26 months. Oppositions can take place at different points in the Martian orbit. Those best for viewing occur when the planet is closest to the Sun, and so also to Earth, because Mars is then at its brightest and largest. Close oppositions occur roughly every 15 years.

Mars spins on its axis once every 24 hours 37 minutes, making a day on Mars only a little longer than an Earth day.

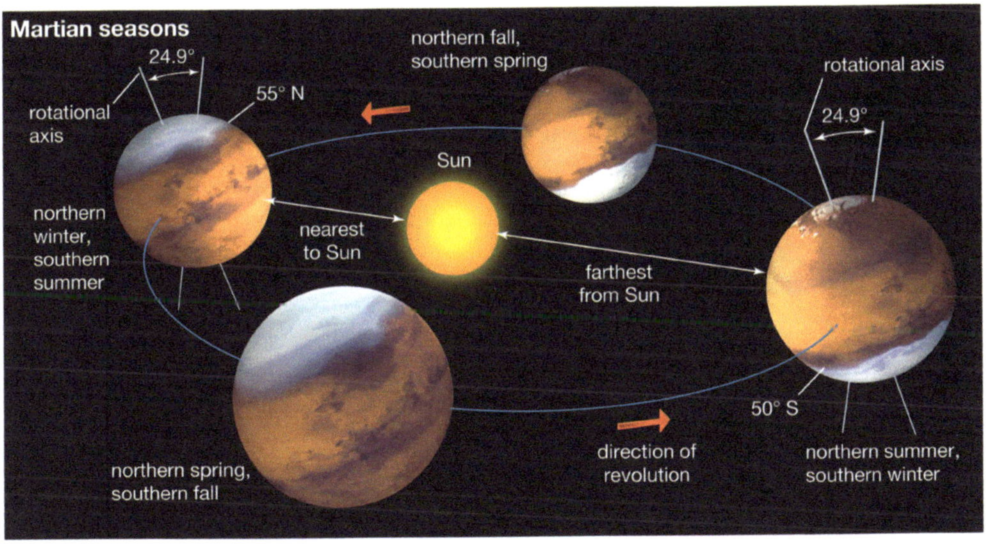




The seasons of Mars, a result of the planet's inclination of 24.9° to its orbital plane. As the seasons change, the polar caps alternately grow and shrink.

Its axis of rotation is inclined to its orbital plane by about 25°, and, as for Earth, the tilt gives rise to seasons on Mars. The Martian year consists of 668.6 Martian solar days, called sols. Because of the elliptical orbit, southern summers are shorter (154 Martian days) and warmer than those in the north (178 Martian days). The situation is slowly changing, however, such that 25,000 years from now the northern summers will be the shorter and warmer ones. In addition, the obliquity, or tilt, of the axis is slowly changing on a roughly one-million-year timescale. During the present epochs the obliquity may range from close to zero, at which times Mars has no seasons, to as high as 45°, when seasonal differences are extreme. Over hundred-million-year timescales the obliquity may reach values as high as 80°.

Mars is a small planet, larger than only Mercury and slightly more than half the size of Earth. It has an equatorial radius of 3,396 km (2,110 miles) and a mean polar radius of 3,379 km (2,100 miles). The mass of Mars is only one-tenth the terrestrial value, and its gravitational acceleration of 3.72 metres (12.2 feet) per second per second at the surface means that objects on Mars weigh a little more than a third of their weight on Earth's surface. Mars has only 28 percent of the surface area of Earth, but, because more than two-thirds of Earth is covered by water, the land areas of the two planets are comparable.

## MARS'S ATMOSPHERE

The Dutch American astronomer Gerard P. Kuiper ascertained from telescopic observations in 1947 that the Martian atmosphere is composed mainly of carbon dioxide. The atmosphere is very thin, exerting less than 1 percent of Earth's atmospheric pressure at the surface. Surface pressures range over a factor of 15 because of the large altitude variations in Mars's topography. Only small amounts of water are present in the atmosphere today. If it all precipitated out, it would form a layer of ice crystals only 10 micrometres (0.0004 inch) thick, which could be gathered into a solid block of ice not much larger than a medium-sized terrestrial iceberg. Despite the small amount of water present, the atmosphere is near saturation, and water-ice clouds are common.

Low-lying clouds and fogs are often observed within topographic depressions—i.e., valleys or craters. Thin clouds are common at the morning terminator (the dividing line between the lit and unlit portions of the planet's disk), and orographic clouds, produced when moist air is lifted over elevated terrain and cooled, form around prominent topographic features such as craters and volcanoes. In winter, westward-moving spiral-shaped storm systems, similar to those on Earth, are seen regularly at midlatitudes. Most of these clouds—in particular, the white clouds seen by the early observers—are composed of water ice.

Dust storms are common on Mars. They can occur at any time but are most frequent in southern spring and summer, when Mars is passing closest to the Sun and surface temperatures are at their highest. Most of the storms are regional in extent and last a few weeks. Every second or third year, however, the dust storms become global. At their peak, dust is carried so high in the atmosphere that only the summits of the loftiest volcanoes—up to 21 km (13 miles) above the planet's mean radius—are visible.

Although too small to be observed from Earth, dust devils have been seen from Mars orbit and at the various spacecraft landing sites. Narrow tracks, thought to be caused by dust devils, are also visible in high-resolution images taken from orbit.

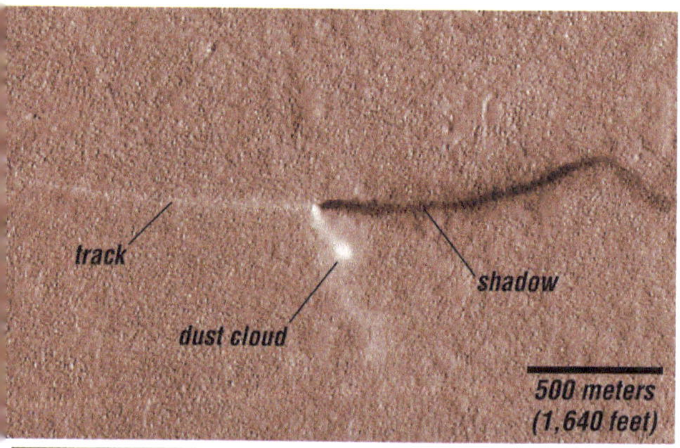


Dust devil in the Amazonis Planitia region of Mars, imaged by Mars Global Surveyor on April 10, 2001.

The characteristic temperature in the lower atmosphere is about 200 kelvins (K; −100 °F, −70 °C), which is generally colder than the average daytime surface temperature of 250 K (−10 °F, −20 °C). These values are in the same range as those experienced on Earth in Antarctica during winter. In summer above a very dark surface, daytime temperatures can peak at about 290 K (62 °F, 17 °C). Above the turbulent layer close to the surface, temperature decreases with elevation at a rate of about 1.5 K (2.7 °F, 1.5 °C) per km (about 2.4 K [4.3 °F, 2.4 °C] per mile) of altitude.

Unlike that of Earth, the atmosphere of Mars experiences large seasonal variations in pressure as carbon dioxide, the main constituent, "snows out" at the winter pole and returns directly to a gas (sublimes) in the spring. Because the southern winter cap is more extensive than the northern, atmospheric pressure reaches a minimum during southern winter when the southern cap is at its largest. The pressure varies annually by 26 percent as some 7.9 trillion metric tons of carbon dioxide leave and reenter the atmosphere seasonally. This is equivalent to a thickness of at least 23 cm (9 inches) of solid carbon dioxide (dry ice) or several metres of carbon dioxide snow averaged over the vast area of the seasonal polar caps.

## COMPOSITION AND SURFACE PRESSURE

Carbon dioxide constitutes 95.3 percent of the atmosphere by weight, nine times the quantity now in Earth's much more massive atmosphere. Much of Earth's carbon dioxide, however, is chemically locked in sedimentary rocks; the amount in the Martian atmosphere is less than a thousandth of the terrestrial total. The balance of the Martian atmosphere consists of molecular nitrogen, water vapour, and noble gases (argon, neon, krypton, and xenon). There are also trace amounts of gases that have been produced from the primary constituents by photochemical reactions, generally high in the atmosphere; these include molecular oxygen, carbon monoxide, nitric oxide, and small amounts of ozone.

Although water is only a minor constituent of the Martian atmosphere (a few molecules per 10,000 at most), primarily because of low atmospheric and surface tempera-

Frost commonly forms at middle and high latitudes on Mars, much like snow on Earth. However, on Mars most frost is carbon dioxide dry ice rather than water ice.

tures, it plays an important role in atmospheric chemistry and meteorology. The Martian atmosphere is effectively saturated with water vapour, yet there is no liquid water present on the surface. The temperature and pressure of the planet are so low that water molecules can exist only as ice or as vapour. Little water is exchanged daily with the surface despite the very cold nighttime surface temperatures.

The global pattern of atmospheric circulation on Mars shows many superficial similarities to that of Earth, but the root causes are very different. Among these differences are the atmosphere's ability to adjust rapidly to local conditions of solar heat input; the lack of oceans, which on Earth have a large resistance to temperature changes; the great range in altitude of the surface; the strong internal heating of the atmosphere because of suspended dust; and the seasonal deposition and release of a large part of the Martian atmosphere at the poles.

Near-surface winds at the Viking and Pathfinder landing sites were usually regular in behaviour and generally light. Average speeds were typically less than 2 metres per second (4.5 miles per hour), although gusts up to 40 metres per second (90 miles per hour) were recorded. Other observations, including streaks of windblown dust and patterns in dune fields and in the many varieties of clouds, have provided additional clues about surface winds.

Global circulation models, which incorporate all the factors understood to influence the behaviour of the atmosphere, predict a strong dependence of winds on the Martian seasons because of the large horizontal temperature gradients associated with the edge of the polar caps in the fall and winter. Strong jet streams with eastward velocities above 100 metres per second (225 miles per hour) form at high latitudes in winter. Circulation is less dramatic in spring and fall, when light winds predominate everywhere. On Mars, unlike on Earth, there is also a relatively strong north-south circulation that transports the atmosphere to and from the winter and summer poles. The general circulation pattern is occasionally unstable and exhibits large-scale wave motions and instabilities: a regular series of rotating high- and low-pressure systems was clearly seen in the pressure and wind records at the Viking lander sites.

Smaller-scale motions and oscillations, driven both by the Sun and by surface topography, are ubiquitous. For example, at the Viking and Pathfinder landing sites, the winds change in direction and speed throughout the day in response to the position of the Sun and the local slope of the land.

Turbulence is an important factor in raising and maintaining the large quantity of dust found in the Martian atmosphere. Dust storms tend to begin at preferred locations in the southern hemisphere during the southern spring and summer. Activity is at first local and vigorous (for reasons yet to be understood), and large amounts of dust are thrown high into the atmosphere. If the amount of dust reaches a critical quantity, the storm rapidly intensifies, and dust is carried by high winds to all parts of the planet. In a few days the storm has obscured the entire surface, and visibility has been reduced to less than 5 percent of normal. The intensification process is evidently short-lived, as atmospheric clarity begins to return almost immediately, becoming normal typically in a few weeks.

## THE SURFACE OF MARS

The character of the Martian terrain has been well established from spacecraft photography and altimetry. Almost the entire planet has been photographed from orbit at a resolution of 20 metres (66 feet) and selected areas at resolutions as high as 20 cm (8 inches). In addition, the laser altimeter on Mars Global Surveyor measured surface elevations for the entire planet, averaged over a circle 300 metres (1,000 feet) across to a vertical accuracy of 1 metre (3.3 feet).

Many maps have been made to illustrate topography, geology, temperature, mineral distributions, and a variety of other data. After Mariner 9 the prime meridian on Mars—the equivalent of the Greenwich meridian

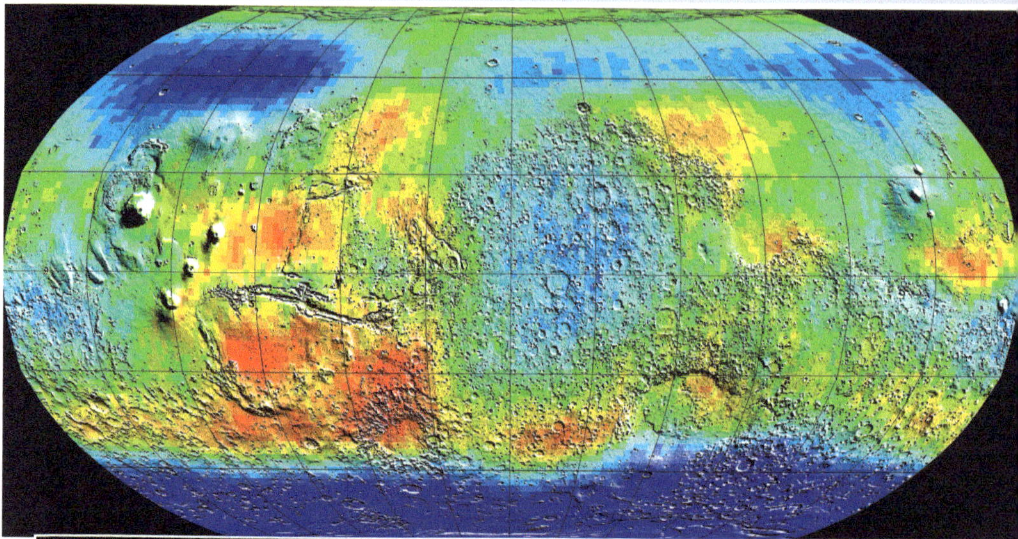

Global map of Mars in epithermal (intermediate-energy) neutrons. Deep blue areas at the high latitudes are suggestive of large reservoirs of water ice below the surface.

on Earth—was defined as passing through a small crater named Airy-0 within the larger crater Airy. Longitude was measured in degrees that increase to the west of this meridian completely around the planet. Later some scientists expressed a preference for a coordinate system with longitude that increases to the east of the prime meridian. Consequently, maps of Mars were published with either or both of these systems.

Despite its small size, Mars has significantly more relief than Earth. The lowest point on the planet, within the Hellas impact basin, is 8 km (5 miles) below the reference level. The highest point, at the summit of the volcano Olympus Mons, is 21 km (13 miles) above the reference level. The elevation range is thus 29 km (18 miles), compared with about 20 km (12.4 miles) on Earth—i.e., from the bottom of the Mariana Trench to the top of Mount Everest. Because Mars has no oceans, a reference level for elevations had to be defined in terms other than sea level. In the early 1970s the elevation at which the atmospheric pressure is 6.1 millibars (about 0.006 of the sea-level pressure on Earth) was set as the reference. When Mars Global Surveyor acquired more-accurate elevation data, a better reference was needed, and the planet's mean radius of 3,389.51 km (2,106.14 miles) was chosen.

One of the most striking aspects of the Martian surface is the contrast between the southern and northern hemispheres. Most of the southern hemisphere is high-standing and heavily cratered, resembling the battered highlands of the Moon. Most of the northern hemisphere is low-lying and sparsely cratered. The difference in mean elevation between the two hemispheres is roughly 6 km (3.7 miles). The topographic boundary between the hemispheres is not parallel to the equator but roughly follows a great circle inclined to it by about 30°. In some places the boundary is broad and irregular; in other places there are steep cliffs.

Some of the most intensely eroded areas on Mars occur along the boundary. Landforms there include outflow channels, areas of collapse called chaotic terrain, and an enigmatic mix of valleys and ridges known as fretted terrain. Straddling the boundary in the western hemisphere is the Tharsis rise, a vast volcanic pile 4,000 km (2,500 miles) across and 8 km (5 miles) above the reference level at its centre. It stands 12 km (7.5 miles) above the northern plains and more than 2 km (1.2 miles) above the surrounding cratered southern highlands. On or near the Tharsis rise are the planet's largest volcanoes. Conspicuously absent in either hemisphere are the types of landforms that on Earth result from plate tectonics—for example, long linear mountain chains similar to the Andes, oceanic trenches, or a global system of interconnected ridges.

The hemispheric dichotomy most likely formed when a large asteroid collided with Mars very early in its history. The resulting northern hemisphere impact crater measures roughly 8,500 by 10,700 km (5,300 by 6,600 miles) across; the object that crashed into Mars would have been more than 2,000 km (1,200 miles) across. Gravity data acquired by Mars Global Surveyor suggest that the Martian crust is much thicker under the southern highlands than under the northern plains.

Results from the Mars Exploration Rovers and from spectrometers on orbiting spacecraft show that the ancient highlands are compositionally distinct from the younger plains. The rover Spirit landed on a basalt plain that may be typical of plains. The rocks on the plains are mostly typical basalts with only thin alteration rinds high in sulfur, chlorine, and other volatile elements. The rinds probably formed by interaction of the basalts with acid fogs. The rover then traveled into the older Columbia Hills, where the rocks are very different. They are mostly basalts and impact breccias, but many are pervasively altered and rich in sulfates and hydrated minerals.

Soils consisting almost entirely of sulfates or silica are also present. Many of the rocks appear to have been permeated by warm volcanic fluids or to have been weathered as a result of warm surface conditions. This mix of rocks and soils may be typical of the highlands in general. The results from orbit tell a similar story. Globally, the plains consist mostly of primary, unaltered basaltic minerals such as olivine and pyroxene. In contrast, alteration minerals such as clays are common throughout the ancient cratered terrain. The results indicate that surface conditions changed dramatically around 3.7 billion years ago. Prior to that time, warm and wet conditions were common and resulted in extensive rock alteration; after that time such conditions were rare, and rock alteration was minor.

## VALLEYS AND LAKES

Most of the ancient cratered terrain is dissected by networks of dry valleys, mostly 1–2 km (0.6–1.2 miles) across and up to 2,000 km (1,200 miles) long. In outline they resemble terrestrial river systems. The valleys almost certainly formed by slow erosion of running water. Many local lowlands have a valley entering and a valley leaving, indicating that the lowland formerly contained a lake. Layered deposits, possibly deposited in lakes, commonly underlie these areas, and deltas are commonly observed where valleys enter the lowlands. Valley networks are rare, although not absent, in the younger, more sparsely cratered areas. Discovery of the valleys in the 1970s was a surprise because of the difficulty of having liquid water at the surface under present conditions. Their common presence in the heavily cratered terrain is another indicator that conditions on early Mars were much warmer and wetter than they are today.

## OUTFLOW CHANNELS AND OCEANS

Large flood channels, termed "outflow channels," are observed incised into the Martian surface in several areas. The channels are much larger than the valley networks, generally being tens of kilometres across and hundreds of kilometres long. Most emerge full-sized from rubble-filled depressions and continue downslope into the northern plains or the Hellas basin in the south. Many of the largest drain from the south and west into Chryse Planitia. These are true channels in that they were once completely filled with flowing water, as opposed to most river valleys, which have never been close

Outflow channels that are believed to have been incised into the Martian surface by floodwaters moving downslope. The channels are roughly 1 km (0.6 mile) deep.

to full but contain a much smaller river channel.

The peak discharges of the floods that cut the larger outflow channels are estimated to have been a hundred to a thousand times the peak discharge of the Mississippi River—truly enormous events. Some of the floods appear to have formed by catastrophic release of water from lakes. Others formed by explosive eruptions of groundwater.

The outflow channels are younger than the valley networks and probably mostly formed when conditions were similar to those that prevail today. Recent discovery of very young outflow channels suggests that they could form today by eruption of groundwater from below the kilometre-thick permanently frozen ground.

## POLAR SEDIMENTS, GROUND ICE, AND GLACIERS

At each pole is a stack of finely layered water-ice-rich sediments about 3 km (2 miles) thick and only a few tens

## SEARCHING FOR LIFE ON MARS

From the beginnings of telescopic observations of Mars, people have speculated about whether life could have started on the planet and what that life might be like. Early observers were concerned mostly with intelligent life, but the focus now is on life's origin, microbial communities, and limits to their survival.

However, several factors subsequently contributed to a more optimistic view. The first is recognition that life can survive in a far wider range of conditions than was formerly thought possible, including near deep-sea vents at temperatures well over 1,000 °C (1,800 °F), in basaltic rocks deep below the surface, and in very saline and acid environments. The second is the discovery that on Earth life started very quickly, possibly before the end of heavy bombardment, which possibly indicates that the origin of life is not an extremely low-probability event but rather will follow if the right conditions are present. The third is mounting evidence that conditions on early Mars, when life arose on Earth, were Earth-like. A fourth factor is recognition that Earth and Mars exchange materials. More than 30 pieces of Mars have been found on Earth, despite the difficulty of distinguishing

Mars rocks from Earth rocks. It is more difficult to get Earth rocks to Mars. Nevertheless, during the period of heavy bombardment, when life may have already started on Earth and conditions on Mars were Earth-like, pieces of Earth may have been transported to Mars. Thus, life may have originated independently on Mars or been seeded from Earth.

of millions of years old. The layering is exposed around the periphery of the sediments and in valleys that spiral out from the poles. In winter the sediments are covered with carbon dioxide frost, but they are exposed in summer. At the north pole they extend southward to 80° latitude. At the south pole their extent is less clearly defined, but they appear to extend farther from the pole than in the north.

The layering is believed to result from variations in the proportion of dust and ice, probably caused by changes in the tilt of the rotational axis (obliquity). At high obliquities water ice is driven off from the poles, probably causing the residual water-ice caps to disappear entirely and the ice to be deposited at lower latitudes. At low obliquities the water-ice caps are at their maximum. Obliquity variations also affect the incidence of dust storms and deposition of dust at the poles.

The deposits have a young age because they have all accumulated since the last period of high obliquity when the previous sediments were removed. One peculiarity of the sediments at the north pole is that they are surrounded by, and perhaps rest upon, a vast dune field rich in the sulfate mineral gypsum.

Under present conditions, at latitudes higher than 40°, ground ice is permanently stable at depths less than 1 metre (3 feet) below the surface because temperatures there never get above the frost point. Above 60° latitude the ice is shallow enough to have been detected from orbit. Ice was also found just below the surface by the Phoenix lander at 68° N. At latitudes higher than 40°, recent impact craters have excavated the surface to depths of more than 2 metres (7 feet), revealing the ground ice. There are also numerous surface features caused by the presence of abundant ground ice. These include polygonally fractured ground similar to that found in terrestrial permafrost regions and a general softening of the terrain, probably caused by ice-abetted flow of the near-surface materials.

A striking characteristic of the 40°–60°-latitude bands indicative of ice is the presence of debris aprons at the base of most steep slopes. Materials shed from the slopes appear to have flowed tens of kilometres away from the slopes, and

Chasma Boreale, a long, flat-floored valley in Mars's northern polar ice cap, in an image captured by the Thermal Emission Imaging System instrument on the Mars Odyssey spacecraft.

ground-penetrating radar shows that the aprons contain large fractions of ice.

During periods of high obliquity, ice driven from the poles accumulated on the surface at lower latitudes, possibly to form glaciers. Modeling of atmospheric circulation suggests that the preferred sites for ice accumulation during these periods are the western slopes of the Tharsis volcanoes and northeast of the Hellas basin. All these locations are rich in flow features and morainelike landforms, which suggests that glaciers were indeed formerly present.

The north polar region also contains the largest area of sand dunes on Mars. The dunes, which occupy the northern part of the plain known as Vastitas Borealis, form a band that almost completely encircles the north polar remnant cap. Interlayering of sand and seasonal carbon dioxide snow can be seen in some locations, indicating that the dunes are active on at least a seasonal timescale.

## THE INTERIOR OF MARS

The interior of Mars is poorly known. Planetary scientists have yet to conduct a successful seismic experiment via spacecraft that would provide direct information on internal structure and so must rely on indirect inferences. The moment of inertia of Mars indicates that it has a central core with a radius of 1,300–2,000 km (800–1,200 miles). Isotopic data from meteorites determined to have come from Mars demonstrate unequivocally that the planet differentiated—separated into a metal-rich core and rocky mantle—at the end of the planetary accretion period 4.5 billion years ago. The planet has no detectable magnetic field that would indicate convection (heat-induced flow) in the core today. Large regions of magnetized rock have been detected in the oldest terrains, however, which suggests that very early Mars did have a magnetic field but that it disappeared as the planet cooled and the core solidified.

Martian meteorites also suggest that the core may be more sulfur-rich than Earth's core and the mantle more iron-rich.

Mars is almost certainly volcanically active today, although at a very low level. Some Martian meteorites, which are all volcanic rocks, show ages as young as a few hundred million years, and some volcanic surfaces on the planet are so sparsely cratered that they must be only tens of millions of years old. Thus, Mars was volcanically active in the geologically recent past, which implies that its mantle is warm and undergoing melting locally.

Mars's gravitational field is very different from Earth's. On Earth, excesses and deficits of mass in the surface crust, corresponding to the presence of large mountains and ocean deeps, respectively, tend to be offset by compensating masses at depth (isostatic compensation). Thus, the pull of gravity on Earth is the same on high mountains as it is over the ocean. This is also true for Mars's oldest terrains, such as the Hellas basin and the southern highlands. The younger terrains, such as the Tharsis and Elysium domes, however, are only partly compensated. Associated with both of these regions are gravity highs—that is, places where the measured gravity is significantly higher than elsewhere because of the large mass of the domes. (Similar areas, called mascons, have been detected and mapped on Earth's Moon.)

Because the gravity over the southern highlands is roughly the same as that over the low-lying northern plains, the southern highlands must be underlain by a thicker crust of material that is less dense than the mantle below it. Estimates of the thickness of the Martian crust range from only 3 km (2 miles) under the Isidis impact basin, which is just north of the equator and east of Syrtis Major, to more than 90 km (60 miles) at the south end of the Tharsis rise.

## THE MOONS OF MARS

Little was learned about the two moons of Mars, Phobos and Deimos, after their discovery in 1877 until orbiting spacecraft observed them a century later. Viking 1 flew to within 100 km (60 miles) of Phobos and Viking 2 to within 30 km (20 miles) of Deimos.

Phobos revolves around Mars once every 7 hours 39 minutes. It moves in an exceptionally close orbit at a mean distance of about 6,000 km (3,700 miles) from the surface—less than twice the planet's radius. It is so near that, without internal strength, it would be torn apart by gravitational (tidal) forces. These forces also slow the motion of Phobos and may ultimately cause the satellite to collide with Mars, possibly in less than 100 million years. Deimos suffers the opposite fate. It moves in a more distant orbit, and tidal forces are causing it to recede from the planet. Phobos and Deimos are not visible from all locations on the planet because of their small size, proximity to Mars, and near-equatorial orbits.

Both moons are irregular chunks of rock, roughly ellipsoidal in shape. Phobos is the larger of the two. Phobos's rugged surface is totally covered with impact craters. The largest, the crater Stickney, is about half as wide as the satellite itself. Its surface also exhibits a widespread system of linear fractures, or grooves, many of which are geometrically related to Stickney. In contrast, the surface of Deimos appears smooth, as its many craters are almost completely buried by fine debris, and it shows no fracture system. The difference in appearance between the two moons is thought to be related to the final disposition of the debris produced by impacts.

In the case of the inner, more massive Phobos, the ejected material either fell back to the surface or, if it left the satellite with enough velocity to go into space, subsequently fell on Mars. For the more-distant, smaller Deimos, debris thrown off the satellite remained in orbit until it was recaptured, sifting down to blanket its surface.

The albedo, or reflectivity, of the surfaces of both moons is very low, similar to that of the most primitive types of meteorites. One theory of the origin of the moons is that they are asteroids that were captured when Mars was forming.

Our inner planet neighbors, Mercury, Venus, and Mars, are particularly interesting to scientists because they can teach us, more so than the outer planets, about the origin and nature of Earth. Not only are the terrestrial planets similar compositionally, they are also relatively close enough that we can visit and study them with spacecraft.

The NASA Messenger launched on August 3, 2004, and completed its mission on April 30, 2015, to study Mercury. It discovered that Mercury is a very tectonically active planet. Mercury, being closest to the Sun, can also teach us about the effects of intense solar radiation on planets.

The European Space Agency's Venus Express spacecraft was launched in November 2005. It started exploring the planet in April 2006 to study Venus's thick atmosphere. Venus raises the question why this planet, which is so similar to Earth in size and mass, is so unlike Earth today.

Many spacecraft have studied Mars, including the rover Curiosity, which is still active at the time of this writing and whose mission is to study whether Mars was ever able to support microbial life. Since Mars has shown us signs that liquid water once flowed on its surface, it offers us one of the greatest prospects of discovering extraterrestrial life.

The more we learn about our terrestrial-planet neighbors, the better we can understand the nature of our own planet and those beyond our solar system. What are the conditions needed for life? How abundant are planets similar to ours in the universe? These are questions that we can perhaps find the answers to in our own celestial backyard.

# GLOSSARY

**accretion** Growth by gradual buildup.

**aurora** A luminous phenomenon that consists of streamers or arches of light appearing in the upper atmosphere of a planet's magnetic polar regions and is caused by the emission of light from atoms excited by electrons accelerated along the planet's magnetic field lines.

**Coriolis effect** The deflection of a moving object that is a result of the Coriolis force.

**density** The mass of a unit volume of a material substance.

**dipole** A pair of electric charges or magnetic poles that are of equal magnitude but opposite sign or polarity, separated by a distance.

**fusion** The union of atomic nuclei to form heavier nuclei resulting in the release of enormous quantities of energy when certain light elements unite.

**general relativity** A theory published by Albert Einstein in 1915 that generalizes Einstein's theory of special relativity and states that gravity is a geometric property of space and time.

**global warming** An increase in Earth's atmospheric and oceanic temperatures widely predicted to occur due to an increase in the greenhouse effect resulting especially from pollution from carbon dioxide emissions.

**lithosphere** Where Earth's uppermost mantle and the crust act mechanically as a single rigid layer.

**lobate** Having curved or scalloped edges.

**magnetosphere** A region surrounding Earth in which charged particles are trapped and their behaviour is dominated by the planet's magnetic field.

**mascons** Areas where particularly dense lavas rose up from the mantle and flooded into basins.

**nebula** A mass of interstellar dust or gas, visible as luminous patches or areas of darkness, depending on the way radiation is absorbed.

**perihelion** The point nearest to the Sun in the path of an orbiting celestial body.

**prograde** Direct motion of the planets around the Sun.

**regolith** An insulating debris layer made of dust and rock fragments ejected from distant impacts on a planet's surface.

**retrograde** Moving backward or in an order that is opposite the usual.

**sidereal** Of, relating to, or expressed in relation to stars or constellations.

**special relativity** A theory published by Albert Einstein in 1905 that is based on the two postulates (1) that the speed of light in a vacuum is constant and independent of the source or observer and (2) that the mathematical forms of the laws of physics are invariant in all inertial systems and which leads to the assertion of the equivalence of mass and energy and of change in mass, dimension, and time with increased velocity.

**subduction** A geologic process in which one edge of one crustal plate is forced below the edge of another.

**tenuous** Long and thin.

**tidal force** The effect of the stretching of a body toward the center of mass of another body due to the gradient in strength of the gravitational field.

**transit** An event where a small astronomical body passes in front of a larger astronomical body.

**tropopause** The topmost portion of the troposphere.

**troposphere** The region on Earth where nearly all water vapour exists and essentially all weather occurs.

**vulcanoids** A hypothetical remnant population of asteroid-sized objects orbiting the Sun inside Mercury's orbit.

## MERCURY

Robert G. Strom and Ann L. Sprague, *Exploring Mercury: The Iron Planet* (2003), by two expert researchers in the field, was written during the development of the Messenger spacecraft mission. J. Kelly Beatty, Carolyn Collins Petersen, and Andrew Chaikin (eds.), *The New Solar System*, 4th ed. (1999), contains several chapters of information related to Mercury, especially in the context of the terrestrial planets. Faith Vilas, Clark R. Chapman, and Mildred Shapley Matthews (eds.), *Mercury* (1988), is a comprehensive collection of technical chapters and overviews covering knowledge of the planet to the time of publication, with an extensive bibliography. Nontechnical treatments of the Mariner 10 mission are found in Bruce Murray and Eric Burgess, *Flight to Mercury* (1977); and James A. Dunne and Eric Burgess, *The Voyage of Mariner 10: Mission to Venus and Mercury*, NASA Special Publication 424 (1978); the latter is a well-illustrated account of the drama surrounding the mission, with pictures of people, instruments, and trajectories plus a large collection of images and maps of Mercury. An excellent collection of Mariner 10 photographs is available in Merton E. Davies et al. (eds.), *Atlas of Mercury* (1976).

## VENUS

Ladislav E. Roth and Stephen D. Wall (eds.), *The Face of Venus: The Magellan Radar-Mapping Mission* (1995), is a good post-Magellan popular-level book on the Venusian surface, with many excellent illustrations. Still informative pre-Magellan popular-level treatments include Garry E. Hunt and Patrick Moore, *The Planet Venus* (1982); and Eric Burgess, *Venus, an Errant Twin* (1985).

The scientific understanding of Venus is definitively and comprehensively summarized in S.W. Bougher, D.M. Hunten, and R.J. Phillips (eds.), *Venus II* (1997), a collection of papers written after the Magellan and Galileo missions. Mikhail Ya. Marov and David H. Grinspoon, *The Planet Venus* (1998), provides an excellent post-Magellan treatment of Venusian geology and most other aspects of the planet. A pre-Magellan overview of Venus's surface is given by Alexander T. Basilevsky and James W. Head III, "The Geology of Venus," *Annual Review of Earth and Planetary Sciences*, 16:295–317 (1988). An interesting collection of papers by Soviet scientists in English on Venus is V.L. Barsukov et al. (eds.), *Venus Geology, Geochemistry, and Geophysics* (1992). The results of major spacecraft missions to Venus are reported in several journals: on Pioneer Venus, *Journal of Geophysical Research*, 85:7573–8337 (1980); V.L. Barsukovet al., "The Geology and Geomorphology of the

Venus Surface as Revealed by the Radar Images Obtained by Veneras 15 and 16," *Journal of Geophysical Research*, pt. B, *Solid Earth and Planets*, 91(B4):D378–D398 (March 30, 1986); *Science*, 253:1457–1612 (Sept. 27, 1991), an issue devoted to the Galileo flyby of Venus; and two issues of *Journal of Geophysical Research*, pt. E, *Planets*, vol. 97, devoted to detailed Magellan mission results: no. 8 (Aug. 25, 1992); and no. 10 (Oct. 25, 1992).

## EARTH

Peter D. Ward and Don Brownlee, *Rare Earth: Why Complex Life is Uncommon in the Universe*, 2nd rev. ed. (2003), lays out for general readers a case for the uncommon nature of planet Earth. Jonathan I. Lunine, *Earth: Evolution of a Habitable World* (1999); and John J.W. Rogers, *A History of the Earth* (1993), provide comprehensive introductions to Earth from, respectively, planetological and geologic perspectives. William K. Hartmann, *The History of Earth: An Illustrated Chronicle of an Evolving Planet* (1991), is a lavishly illustrated introduction. A graduate-level text comprising excellent chapters on its subject matter is Robin M. Canup and Kevin Righter (eds.), *Origin of the Earth and Moon* (2000). A popular and balanced account of the physical causes of mass extinctions is given in Charles Frankel, *The End of the Dinosaurs: Chicxulub Crater and Mass*

*Extinctions* (1999; originally published in French, 1996). The periodical *Scientific American* (monthly) is an excellent and accessible source for the latest thinking on Earth and planetary processes; for example, a good description of plate tectonics is found in Ian W.D. Dalziel, "Earth Before Pangea," 272(1):58–63 (January 1995). The *State of the World* report (annual), published by the Worldwatch Institute, provides authoritative updates on Earth's vital signs for the general reader.

## MARS

Donald Goldsmith, *The Hunt for Life on Mars* (1997), describes the events that led to the controversial claims for evidence of life in the Martian meteorite ALH84001. John Noble Wilford, *Mars Beckons: The Mysteries, the Challenges, the Expectations of Our Next Great Adventure in Space* (1990), provides a general introduction. All aspects of Mars science are addressed in Hugh H. Kieffer et al. (eds.), *Mars* (1992), a huge, comprehensive technical summary of existing knowledge. Victor R. Baker, *The Channels of Mars* (1982), is a well-illustrated discussion of how these features came about and their implications for the history of Mars. Michael H. Carr, *The Surface of Mars* (1981), is a profusely illustrated survey of scientists' perception of Mars after the Viking missions, and *Water on Mars* (1996) discusses the role that water has played in the evolution of the Martian surface. Volumes of papers detailing the results of the various Mars spacecraft missions appear in the *Journal of Geophysical Research*: for Viking, 82, no. 28 (1977); for Mars Pathfinder, 104, no. E4 (1999); and for Mars Global Surveyor, 106, no. E4 (2001). These results are summarized in several excellent papers in *Nature*, 412:207–253 (July 12, 2001).

# INDEX